An Illustrated Tour of the 1879 Anglo-Zulu Battlefields

An Illustrated Tour of the 1879 Anglo-Zulu Battlefields

Adrian Greaves

Pen & Sword
MILITARY

First published in Great Britain in 2023 by
Pen & Sword Military
An imprint of Pen & Sword Books Limited
Yorkshire – Philadelphia

ISBN 978 1 39904 068 6

Typeset by Mac Style
Printed in the UK by CPI Group (UK) Ltd, Croydon, CR0 4YY.

MIX
Paper | Supporting
responsible forestry
FSC
www.fsc.org   FSC® C013604

Pen & Sword Books Limited incorporates the imprints of After the Battle,
Atlas, Archaeology, Aviation, Discovery, Family History, Fiction, History,
Maritime, Military, Military Classics, Politics, Select, Transport, True Crime,
Air World, Frontline Publishing, Leo Cooper, Remember When, Seaforth
Publishing, The Praetorian Press, Wharncliffe Local History, Wharncliffe
Transport, Wharncliffe True Crime and White Owl.

For a complete list of Pen & Sword titles please contact

PEN & SWORD BOOKS LIMITED
47 Church Street, Barnsley, South Yorkshire, S70 2AS, England
E-mail: enquiries@pen-and-sword.co.uk
Website: www.pen-and-sword.co.uk
or
PEN AND SWORD BOOKS
1950 Lawrence Rd, Havertown, PA 19083, USA
E-mail: uspen-and-sword@casematepublishers.com
Website: www.penandswordbooks.com

Contents

Introduction

The purpose of this book is to give the reader a perceptive overview of the causes and battles of the 1879 Anglo-Zulu War which commenced with the British defeat at Isandlwana and the defence of Rorke's Drift. For twenty-five years the author regularly visited the numerous battlefields of Zululand, where he worked as an accredited guide and guest speaker, escorting over 1,000 overseas visitors and corporate groups around the far-flung and fascinating battlefields of Zululand. I had the privilege of accompanying several of his tours while conducting my own research into Lieutenant Harford's role in Zululand. His tours regularly visited many unique and important 'off the beaten track' locations, for which his maps were invaluable.

This book's maps and illuminating observations are taken from the author's personal on-site lecture maps and notes he used across the battlefields. The maps include many little-known details of the fierce and bloody battles that were fought in this short campaign. It was a war that lasted only six months and witnessed two separate British invasions of Zululand and, while volumes have been written on the subject, such illustrative maps were able to give visitors an even better insight and understanding of many Anglo-Zulu War events.

Dr David Payne

Harford – The Writings, Photographs and Sketches. David Payne, published by The Ultimatum Tree Ltd., 2008.

Points to note

1. **The maps**. The original maps more easily enabled visitors to orientate themselves, and to better understand each battlefield's layout and the chronology of so many complex and frequently fast-moving events. The maps refer to a savage war; they detail vicious battles and the brutal death of many participants. Accordingly I would remind visitors that, whilst both

sides fought a deadly and vicious war, participants on both sides did so in the belief that what they were doing was right.

2. **Incidents and movements.** Each map's events are numbered in chronological order, showing the known sequence of events portrayed. Zulu locations are shown as black dots, their attacks as black arrows and their retreats as white arrows. British movements, engagements and locations are in light grey. British retreats are shown as grey hatched arrows.

3. **Timings.** Timings throughout the campaign are ambiguous as they are taken from written accounts and reports, most of which are the result of some collusion, helpful or otherwise. Few officers had watches, and no record exists of campaign timings ever being synchronised or coordinated. At best, recorded timings are casual and approximate. For example, the arrival of Colonel Durnford at Isandlwana was witnessed by Colonel Pulleine and his headquarters staff officers, yet a perusal of their messages and survivors' reports of this crucial event reveal more than a dozen different recorded times, covering a three-hour time span. For the same reason, timings of significant events at Rorke's Drift vary by up to four hours.

4. **Locations.** Maps of the day were inaccurate or guesswork, mainly because much of the terrain was still unexplored.

5. **Maps or accounts.** The naming of locations, such as Helpmakaar, Dundee, or any location away from Durban, might suggest a thriving community. The reality was rarely more than a few flimsy homes with a scattering of small farms on nearby hills.

6. **British or English.** Throughout this period, the term 'English' was used in military documents to denote British troops from the UK.

7. **The eclipse.** Any eclipse was unrecorded contemporaneously.

8. **Intelligence**. By 1878, apart from India, there was no meaningful flow of military intelligence between London and the Empire. During that year, three British armies invaded Afghanistan, beginning the second Anglo-Afghan War; further hotspots such as India and the fear of Russia's growing influence, concentrated diplomatic minds. South Africa was pushed to the sideline.

Map Key

British locations and features   =   Durban and ⬤

British advances   =   ➡

British retreats   =   ⬅

Zulu features   =   ⬤

Zulu advances   =   ➡

Zulu retreats   =   ⬅

Boer attacks   =   ➡

Overview

Britain's perilous state

In March 1881, the defeated Zulu king was held a prisoner at the Cape when he dictated a letter to the governor, Sir Hercules Robinson. Via his interpreter, King Cetshwayo poignantly stated:

> Mpande [Cetshwayo's father] did you no wrong. I have done you no wrong, therefore you must have some other object in view in invading my land.

That 'other object' has remained elusive not only to the Zulus but to the majority of historians and writers on Zulu affairs. Popular authors dealing with the causes of the Anglo-Zulu War still rely heavily or exclusively on the Zulu refusal to comply with the British ultimatum of December 1878 as being the rationale for the war. These writers' sources are invariably based on contemporary accounts, which, being written by the victors, were highly subjective; there were important reputations to preserve and sufficient scapegoats abounded, some conveniently dead, to explain the unexplainable rapid succession of British military defeats and setbacks. Modern accounts of the war tend to rely on the official and worthy *Narrative of Field Operations*, but the *Narrative* refrained from any allusion of controversy. Perhaps the most honest explanation can be credited to Professor John P.C. Laband and P.S. Thompson's *Field Guide to the War in Zululand and Defence of Natal 1879* in which they state, 'there is still no general agreement on the causes of the Anglo Zulu War'.

In order to understand the strange but true historical background to this war, one must, briefly, consider the birth of the developing and innovative British government's foreign policy, known as 'confederation'. This policy was designed to deal with the growing military threat to Britain's far-flung colonies, not from the Zulus, but from Russia and Germany. Its purpose was defensive and primarily to enable 'Fortress England' to protect and administer all her overseas colonies, including South Africa, from progressively unwelcome foreign interference. During the 1870s, confederation was becoming an increasingly important factor in British foreign strategy worldwide following its earlier successful implementation in lands as distant as India, Australia, The Leeward Islands and, most recently and successfully, Canada, all under the guidance of Lord Carnarvon, then Britain's Colonial Secretary.

It was in the light of this particular success that confederation was considered essential for Britain's developing interests in southern Africa, especially with its diverse and often antagonistic populations or unwelcome visits by Russian gunboats. Theoretically, once unified, the area could then develop its own military system, albeit supervised by British officers, which neatly solved the problem of Britain supplying and maintaining hugely expensive Imperial garrisons for distant peacekeeping roles. With such a policy, these areas soon flourished; they even became self-supporting and in due course rewarded Britain with the massive bonus of the home nation being able to enjoy highly profitable trade.

This policy is important to our understanding of the Anglo-Zulu War because it directly influenced a number of complex issues that closely related to the period leading immediately to the war. Then, as now in the modern world, the importance of sea routes can hardly be underestimated. Since the mid-1850s, while the British/Russian Crimean War progressed, officials in India led by a senior imperial administrator of India and Zanzibar, Henry Bartle Edward Frere (later known as Bartle Frere or Frere), began to ponder the vulnerability of Britain's world trade caused by belligerent foreign raiding ships (privateers) and the blatant attention of Russian warships to Britain's vital but unprotected overseas trade routes.

After bringing East African slavery to a close, Frere then planned the defence of Imperial India, reliant on the Royal Navy's control of sea routes to India. He was also concerned by the real and growing threat of a Russian land incursion into India via Afghanistan.

In early 1863, Russian interference spread further across the Pacific when the flagship of the Russian Pacific Squadron, Rear Admiral Popov's *Bogatyr*, officially made a 'friendly' but probing visit to Melbourne. Then in June 1864, the Australian authorities discovered from a dissident Polish naval officer serving on the *Bogatyr*, Władysław Zbyszewski, that Popov had received orders, to be followed in the event of conflict, to attack any British naval ships positioned near the Australian shore. The plan also included the shelling and destruction of Melbourne, along with coastal batteries at Sydney and Hobart. Similar anti-British attack orders were later discovered to have been given to the Atlantic Squadron under Admiral Lessovsky, who had been sent to New York at the same time.

Theoretically, Britain's Royal Navy had already assumed strategic responsibility for the Indian Ocean, although the British had earlier been surprised in October 1866 when the aggressive Confederate USS *Shenandoah* unexpectedly arrived in Bombay Harbour under cover of darkness. Being steam driven, she was one of the fastest warships of the time and had already seized or sunk over thirty-five vessels in just over a year while circumnavigating the globe. An alarmed Frere then wrote to the Secretary of State for India of the danger presented by this vessel:

> She might have dropped in on us in times of war as in peace and we have nothing to meet her nearer than Trincomalee a thousand miles distant and not in telegraphic communication with us … a vessel like this could extort a ransom of many millions sterling… The captain could have no difficulty in dropping a shell on the mint or bank building as a hint to hasten payment.
>
> 2 October 1866, Martineau Vol. 1 p.464

Apart from her dominant home naval power, Britain had already developed overseas naval bases around the world where its warships could refuel, initially with coal and later with oil. They could replenish with fresh water and provisions and carry out essential maintenance without having to return all the way to Britain. These locations also protected Britain's important overseas interests; its South African base in Simon's Town theoretically protected the vital passage around the Cape of Good Hope to India, the Far East and Australia while Bahrain controlled the sea lane through the Persian Gulf; Trincomalee in Ceylon controlled the sea lane across the North Indian Ocean, and Singapore protected the southern entrance to the Straits of Malacca. The core of British naval strategy was to prevent rival powers from establishing a naval base anywhere in the Indian Ocean. Clearly, without access to fuel and supplies from a friendly base, no hostile warship could operate in this oceanic expanse for any length of time.

The opening of the Suez Canal in 1869, together with the laying of undersea telegraph cables from Britain to her Indian Ocean bases in the 1870s, the advent of steam-propelled and propeller-driven warships, the establishment of coaling stations, dry docks and armament depots in the naval bases all combined to underpin Britain's Indian Ocean strategy. The core of this strategy was to maintain the strongest ships of her fleet in British waters and deploy smaller, older and weak, squadrons in distant bases. As soon as a threat was reported to Britain's sea lines of communication, warships of the appropriate power and speed would be directed by telegraph to converge on the threat. In the event of a prolonged confrontation, reinforcements would be moved from elsewhere.

But this policy left the Cape and South Africa vulnerable and totally unprotected, worse, there was no telegraph to South Africa. In 1875 Vice Admiral Hornby complained, 'We are sadly deficient in ships to furnish reliefs to those on foreign stations and we have no reserve whatsoever.' Britain's Royal Navy, with many of its active warships still resembling Nelson's navy, was understandably known as being in 'the dark ages'. By 1876, just three years before the Anglo-Zulu War, Russia's growing influence was blatant; the British cabinet collectively became aware of South Africa's vulnerability when it was minuted by the Colonial Committee charged with considering the protection of British sea routes.

If such a misfortune as a war with Russia were to occur, it would be everything to have it in our power to deal a sudden and crushing blow in Asia. Every precaution therefore that can be properly adopted will be wise.

Carnarvon to Salisbury, 1876

The British government knew only too well that defences of the Cape were non-existent. They were also greatly concerned that the Royal Navy was unable to intercept or deter the Russian Navy in the event of a Russian blockade of the Cape. Then, in 1878, an internal government report confirmed a Russian naval squadron had sailed from Europe completely undetected until it arrived in America. Had it gone to the Cape it could have easily overwhelmed any British vessels, Cape Town would have been defenceless, and worse, British ships would have been denied refuelling and supplies. Anxiety in parliament increased when, in the same year, British intelligence discovered that Russian crews were in the US to acquire surplus American cruiser battleships suitable for coastal raiding, with another fifty smaller warships under negotiation.

Britain's leaders remained complacent, knowing they possessed the most powerful land army. In 1878 the British Army fielded over 100 line regiments, each made up of eight companies. The first twenty-five regiments of the line, mainly those serving overseas, had two battalions, the second battalion's role was to maintain a steady flow of home recruits. Army tactics had changed little since Waterloo, with British troops still in bright red uniform jackets and trained to fight in squares using controlled volley fire against opponents. Meanwhile, their European counterparts had begun to retrain with smaller attacking groups, using the terrain and camouflage to reduce their visibility. Politically, the indignity of the Crimean War was still fresh in British minds, after Britain had sought to prevent the Russian navy gaining access between the Black Sea and the Mediterranean. Politicians now sought to strengthen Britain's colonies, which theoretically united each colony for mutual defence to offset the growing aggressive influence of Russia, America and, of increasing importance, Germany, where Bismarck's Anglophobic campaign was encouraging a fledgling German colonial movement and made sure that its first colonies in Africa would be in areas the British regarded as their own.

During his service in India, Frere had especially considered Cape Town to be 'utterly defenceless' and had long since expressed his concern over the vulnerability of the Cape to enemy warships since witnessing the construction of the Suez Canal when passing through on his return to England from India. Frere worried over the possibility of anti-British threats to British controlled South and East Africa. He noted:

> I have no doubt that a telegraph to the Cape would be very valuable, both from an Imperial and a Colonial point of view and … still more valuable for military reasons…I am bound to say I think the telegraph is important, for at any moment the Cape may become to us a station of first class value.

Frere's main thrust was to protect the Cape, which, in turn, was the key port to protect Britain's vital trade routes with India. The possibility of Russian interference also weighed heavily on the Chancellor of the Exchequer, Sir Stafford Northcote, who commented:

If such a misfortune as a war with Russia were to occur, it would be everything to have it in our power to deal a sudden and crushing blow in Asia. Every precaution therefore that can properly be adopted will be wise.

An increasingly worried Lord Carnarvon, Colonial Secretary, had meanwhile obtained permission from Prime Minister Disraeli to send Frere to South Africa, primarily to ensure the defence of the colony and its two main ports, Cape Town and Durban. Frere's administrative role was also to effect the unification of Southern African territories under British rule and to bring into line the militantly chaotic and bankrupt Boer Republic to the north of the Cape. Frere's sincere and dominating belief was that war with Russia was inevitably looming and that South African ports were vulnerable to attack by Russian warships and privateers. He was also now aware of the previously unanticipated threat of rebellion by the disgruntled neighbouring Boer Republic.

Undaunted, Frere arrived at the Cape on 31 March 1877, accompanied by his wife and four daughters, and found his family accommodation and Government House offices 'run down'. Nevertheless, he set to work and instigated a survey to see how the harbour of Cape Town could be defended. Nearby Simon's Town was more easily defended, but it was a week away for marching soldiers, or a day's sailing, even if a British ship was present. Frere promptly gave orders for four gun batteries to be constructed, with an additional floating battery to be positioned at the entrance of the harbour.

But from the beginning, Frere was also forced on a daily basis to contend with the growing reality of a cascade of unexpected problems, including a Xhosa rebellion, the strong likelihood of a Boer rebellion stoked by Germany and, or, a Zulu attack on the Transvaal, all combined with his priority of thwarting Russian warships interdicting the Cape shipping and landing marines. Still, Frere was not a man to be deterred by such difficulties. On his arrival in Cape Town, he had immediately improved the defences of the port areas against a naval raid, despite official foot dragging in London. However, in a 'state of uncertainty and anxiety', regarding the Treaty of Stefano, he said. 'I think the ultimate result must be war'. Sir Michael Hicks-Beach, Secretary of State for the Colonies, was apt to downgrade the seriousness of a Russian threat to the Cape, and wrote to Frere accordingly:

> I hope your harbours and stores at Cape Town are to some extent protected: at least sufficiently so to defeat the only kind of attack likely to be made on them by a stray cruiser or privateer.

Frere knew only too well that such 'stray cruisers' were not to be despised. The *Shenandoah* had wreaked havoc when circumnavigating the globe operating in waters as diverse as the Southern oceans and the North Pacific and was fast enough to travel 300 miles in twenty-four hours, thus allowing it to attack civilian shipping off Cape Town and disappear before the Royal Navy could be alerted. If, as Frere feared, Russian cruisers did become active, merchant shipping would simply not leave port, trade would dry up, insurance rates rocket, and the inevitable outcry would necessitate the diversion of scarce naval resources from other theatres. Frere responded with a warning that was a repeat of his earlier concerns for the security of Bombay.

> I wish it were…easy to defend our ports from privateers, should you be unable to avert a European war. The subject was one of the first things I attended to when I came out…. This was only managed by commencing work at my own risk…. But Table Bay is still open to any vessel with a single rifled gun, and a privateer might levy a contribution from our Banks before a man-of-war could come to our help. The Russians know this well, and when their squadron was here two or three years ago, the officers used to tell their partners at balls that 'they did not intend to wait to be taken by the English Channel or Mediterranean fleets, but to pay visits to the Cape and Indian ports where they would levy contributions, on their way to Petrapaulovski!'. Meantime the enclosed Memo shows the guns Col. Hassard asks for, and if you could only get the War Office to send us some of them…I could make a beginning and not run the risk of having to report your flag hauled down and a contribution of half a million or more levied by some wretched Alabama cruiser or privateer.

Meanwhile, just as war with Russia seemed imminent, rumours and spicy gossip were rife at all levels of the British government when it was discovered that, somehow, Russian agents had access to British military secrets. A major scandal then erupted when it was discovered that Lady Derby, the wife of Colonial Foreign Secretary, Lord Edward Henry Stanley, Secretary of State for Foreign

Affairs, was having a clandestine relationship with a senior Russian diplomat. Lady Derby mixed freely with both British diplomats and ministers when it was discovered she had passed highly secret British cabinet naval material to the Russian government via the Russian ambassador to London, Pyotr Shuvalov. Queen Victoria was informed and, not amused, she instructed her chaplain to write to Lady Derby. It was an unusual royal intervention that resulted in Lord Derby's swift resignation in 1878 as foreign secretary. In open parliament Lord Blake commented that…

> Derby surely must be the only Foreign Secretary in British history to reveal the innermost secrets of the cabinet to the ambassador of a foreign power in order to frustrate the presumed intentions of his own Prime Minister.

The new Russian shipbuilding programme, adopted in the late 1870s, coincided with the Russian naval strategy of open-ocean sea denial, in which the Russian Navy was to have the capacity to engage enemy forces in the high seas. Russian warships were already undertaking exploratory long-range deployments into the Indian Ocean and the Persian Gulf. Politically, the Russian naval presence in the main oceans of the world greatly increased Russia's international prestige and helped to strengthen the country's authority in those regions.

In 1878 Frere received news from Theophilus Shepstone, Natal Secretary for Native Affairs, that due to the recent crash of the Boer economy and the threat of an attack against the Boers by either or both of the adjacent Pedi and Zulu nations, the Boer government had reluctantly agreed to British annexation, and its concomitant protection. Not all Boers were prepared to accept annexation and within days, a deputation of Boers, led by Paul Kruger, set sail for London to argue against the British move. International politics then took a turn for the worse; Russia declared war on Turkey, which strengthened Frere's fear of growing Russian influence, especially as he knew South Africa had no telegraphic communication with the outside world. Frere watched the breakdown in relations between Britain and Russia coinciding with the sailing of a Russian squadron of warships that had slipped unseen into the North Atlantic, and whose whereabouts were unknown to the Royal Navy – until the Russian vessels arrived in the USA. Frere reasoned that, if the Russians instead sailed directly to the Cape, their arrival there would have been unopposed – and the Royal Navy would have then been unable to intervene or refuel. Indeed, in April 1878, the government were well aware Russian naval crews were already in the USA to collect three cruisers, believed to be intended for mischief in the Mediterranean, where they could interfere with passage through the Suez Canal.

For Frere, his difficulties then progressively went from bad to worse. North of the Cape, the Boers were openly taking initial steps to gain access to the Indian Ocean, thereby becoming independent of any British control or interference. They were already in the process of seizing prime farming land in Zululand, to the fury of the Zulus. The threat of rebellion by the disgruntled neighbouring Boer Republic began to outweigh Frere's fears about Russian interference. His masterstroke, albeit temporary, was to turn a blind eye to the Boers' expansion into Zululand's rich farmland and instead protect the Boer farmers by neutralizing the Zulus with a British invasion of Zululand.

Such an invasion was attractive to Frere. Apart from pacifying the Boers, the Zulus were blocking British progress to the north, and their defeat would facilitate confederation, and such a display of force would certainly impress other Bantu nations who might consider making a stand against British expansion. Invasion would overturn the Zulu king by eradicating his military potential and free a valuable source of labour for growing British and Boer commercial activities.

Frere ordered his general commanding British forces in South Africa, Sir Frederic Thesiger (shortly to become Lord Chelmsford), to proceed to Natal to secretly prepare his forces for an immediate and quick war against the Zulus. There were also important personal considerations for both Frere and Chelmsford; success for Frere would strengthen his already glittering career, and for Chelmsford, an early defeat of the Zulu army would be popular and ensure him an heroic return to England. Meanwhile, Frere requested additional imperial troops, ostensibly to protect Natal and the Boer families still within the area. He knew full well that Hicks Beach's official reply would take several months to reach him.

Eventually, on 11 December 1878, Zulu representatives were summoned to the site of a shady tree on the Natal bank of the Tugela River – today a neglected national monument under a motorway bridge – to be informed of the decision of a contrived British Boundary Commission's deliberations to undermine the Zulu king. John Shepstone, brother of the Secretary for Native

Affairs, Sir Theophilus Shepstone, represented the British officials, while King Cetshwayo sent three of his senior *indunas* together with eleven chieftains and their retainers to listen to the findings. Writing was unknown to the Zulus, who were nevertheless accomplished at memorising even lengthy speeches and which probably accounts for the number of senior Zulu representatives, who would have to corroborate each other when they reported to Cetshwayo.

The findings were relayed to the Zulu officials but in heavily worded terms designed to cause added confusion. The hitherto secret ultimatum was then read to the astonished Zulus who then anxiously set off to report the impossible terms of the ultimatum to Cetshwayo, knowing the king's propensity to execute the bringers of bad news.

The main requirements of the ultimatum included:

Conditions to be fully met within twenty days:
1. The surrender to the British of the Swazi Chief, Mbilini, (for cattle raiding).
2. The surrender of Chief Sihayo's two sons (for crossing the river border into Natal, abducting and then murdering two of Sihayo's adulterous wives) plus a fine of 500 cattle.
3. A fine of 100 cattle for having molested two British surveyors, Deighton and Smith, at a border crossing.

Conditions to be fully met within thirty days:
1. A number of prominent Zulus were to be surrendered for trial (no names were specified).
2. Summary executions were forbidden.
3. The Zulu army was to disband.
4. The Zulu military system was to be abandoned.
5. Every Zulu was to be free to marry.
6. Missionaries were to be readmitted to Zululand without let or hindrance.
7. A British resident official was to oversee Zulu affairs.
8. Any dispute involving a European was to be dealt with under British jurisdiction.

In the meantime, the freshly assembled British invasion force was already advancing towards the borders of Zululand in total confidence that Cetshwayo could not comply with the ultimatum. Hicks Beach's reply finally reached Frere and it was, as Frere anticipated, an indication that Hicks Beach was uninterested in southern Africa. It contained little more than a request that caution must be exercised. The reply read:

> Her Majesty's Government are [*sic*] not prepared to comply with a request for reinforcement of troops. All the information that has hitherto reached them with respect to the position of affairs in Zululand appears to justify a confident hope that by the exercise of prudence and by meeting the Zulus in a spirit of forbearance and reasonable compromise, it will be possible to avert the very serious evil of a war with Cetshwayo.

Frere interpreted Hicks Beach's reply as inferring authority to initiate a local war and, once started, the British government was powerless to stop him. It took at least ten weeks for a message to travel to London and back; his exploitation of the delay, on the grounds of the tension and urgency he had personally created, was blatant.

For King Cetshwayo, five years of comparative peace were about to end. During his reign a number of minor incidents had occurred along his distant borders, but they were petty and of no real concern to the British. Cetshwayo was in total control of his country, and he maintained his authority with an available army of over 50,000 warriors spread over at least 30 *amabutho* regiments.

By the end of September 1878, Cetshwayo was fully aware that events were rapidly moving beyond his control, and from his royal homestead on the rolling Mahlabathini plain, he mobilized the Zulu army to assemble before him. He also ordered wild animal hunts to be held along the borders of the neighbouring territories, and they were instructed to ensure that they were observed by Shepstone's spies. By the time the ultimatum reached Cetshwayo, most of the *amabutho* were already gathered, and the ritual preparations for war began. Notwithstanding soothing reassurances from Shepstone, Cetshwayo was not to be caught off balance. Shrewdly, he decided to wait and watch. He sent a number of *induna* emissaries to implore British restraint, but on presentation of their credentials, they were arrested and imprisoned.

Cetshwayo knew exactly where the British were amassing their forces and correctly presumed their objective. Perhaps because Chelmsford was accompanying the centre column, Cetshwayo singled it out as being the most dangerous force. The time for peaceful negotiation had passed; both sides were ready for war.

The Boers watched on, biding their time. It was fortunate for Britain that, by late 1878, the Russian world-wide naval threat had subsided.

The causes of the Anglo-Zulu War can be summarised as follows:

1. To further British policy of Confederation throughout southern Africa.

    Confederation will involve, we hope, self defence, which will remove the liability under which we labour of spending our blood and money upon these wretched Kaffir [*sic*] quarrels in South Africa.
                          Lord Cadogan Hansard, 25 March 1879

2. To subdue the Zulu in order to…

    a. win favour with the Boers: (over the issue of boundary disputes, an Anglo-Zulu War was preferable to an Anglo-Boer war);
    b. repress widespread black resistance to expanding Boer domination; and
    c. prevent the Zulus from blocking British progress and expansion to the north.

3. To gain personal prestige for Frere and, to a lesser degree, Chelmsford.

4. To free Zulu manpower resources for labour hungry European commercialism.*

    * Sir Theophilus Shepstone wrote:

    Had Cetshwayo's 30,000 warriors been in time changed to labourers working for wages, Zululand would have been a prosperous, peaceful country instead of what it is now, a source of perpetual danger to itself and its neighbours.
                                        Letter dated 1878

Without doubt, the Boer/Zulu confrontation up to 1878 was steadily escalating to the point of an unnecessary full scale war. At the same time, the British government in London had been duped into falsely believing that there was a serious risk of King Cetshwayo's Zulus sweeping across the long and unprotected Zululand border and invading British controlled Natal. In reality, there was no such threat.

In an astonishing act of over-confidence, Frere and Chelmsford pushed ahead with their plan to invade Zululand and deliberately ignored the implications of their recent failed expedition to attack King Sekhukhune's Pedi people in the neighbouring Transvaal – with its embarrassing drubbing of the British invaders. The pair nevertheless authorised the invasion of Zululand and sent Britain to war against this hitherto friendly, if little understood, nation. Their enthusiasm was remarkable, as British intelligence of Zulu military strength was desperately inaccurate and as misleading as the ambiguous traders' maps they were about to rely on.

But what could go wrong? After all, Britain was a highly industrialised nation with a modern, well-equipped and trained army, seeking nothing more than to subdue a seemingly chaotic, uneducated, ill-equipped and inexperienced native population, whose only offence was a minor degree of insignificant non-cooperation. The blunder by Frere and Chelmsford was enormous; these two highly placed and experienced British officials committed Britain to a humiliating, expensive and savage war with tragic loss of life on both sides. Worse still, the war accentuated the British Army's previously unknown deficiencies, some of which had already been highlighted by its failed campaign against King Sekhukhune. And so, after the successful displays of defiance against both the Boers and British by Sekhukhune, Cetshwayo and his Zulu nation defiantly stood their ground when Britain was committed by Frere and Chelmsford to invade Zululand just a few weeks later in January 1879.

At the conclusion of the Zulu campaign, instead of returning home, British forces recovering from fighting the Zulus had to be recommitted to a renewed campaign against Sekhukhune's defiant Pedi people. Then, in June 1879, the British made their second insignificant attempt at subduing Sekhukhune with an inadequate force under the command of Colonel Lanyon. This attempt also failed due to a lack of manpower, supplies and a will to fight. At this point Lord Wolseley took command and personally led his battle-hardened troops to finally deal with Sekhukhune. The campaign was successful and left the British free to tackle the fermenting Boer Transvaal rebellion. Encouraged by several British defeats during the Zulu war, the Boers commenced the first Anglo-Boer war. They began by attacking, while showing the white flag of truce, an unprotected British column, complete with families, en route to Pretoria. But that's another story for the end of this book.

The Zulus were eventually defeated at Ulundi, but at an enormous price, and at the cost of Britain's reputation. A direct consequence of the 1964 film *Zulu* is that the war is still widely perceived as exciting, even stirring, and certainly memorable. Therefore, the enduring general public perception is that it was a war fought by a handful of brave redcoats against the savage Zulus; few know why it was fought and fewer still understand its bitter consequences.

The Anglo-Zulu War itself is a remarkable story of classic heroism of both the invading British soldier and the African warrior fighting to keep invaders from his lands. Without doubt, both sides fought in the belief that what they were doing was right. The war's consequences eventually brought down the British government and left Zululand in chaos. Whatever view one has of Zulu history, it cannot be denied that by the time the Anglo-Zulu War commenced, successive Zulu kings had efficiently controlled the development of Zulu social organization and ensured a comparatively healthy and prosperous population.

Timescale leading to the Anglo-Zulu War:

1869   Britain, France and Italy take joint control of the finances of bankrupt Tunisia.
British explorer Samuel Baker annexes the southern Sudan, or Equatoria, on behalf of the khedive of Egypt.

1871   18-year-old British entrepreneur, Cecil Rhodes, on a temporary visit to South Africa, arrives in the new diamond town of Kimberley.

1874   The southern region of present-day Ghana becomes a British colony, to be known as the Gold Coast.

1875   The beginning of the Balkan crisis, which showed the vulnerability of the Suez Canal to Russian influence and British colonies. India, Australia and South Africa were especially vulnerable.

1876   The chaotic government finances of Egypt are placed under joint French and British control.

India becomes the 'Jewel in the Crown' of Queen Victoria when Benjamin Disraeli secures for her the title 'Empress of India'.

1877 Britain annexes the Boer Republic in the Transvaal.

1878 Three British armies invade Afghanistan, beginning the second Anglo-Afghan War.

1878 Britain invades independent South African Sekhukhuneland and prepares for the invasion of Zululand.

1879 Britain invades Zululand.

Chapter 1

The 1878 British Attack Against King Sekhukhune and his Role in Precipitating the Anglo-Zulu War of 1879

Background

Sekhukhuneland, in the Transvaal to the north of Zululand, was just 120 miles east of Pretoria and north-west of the Swazi kingdom. Its Pedi people under King Sekhukhune had long been in a state of rebellion against anyone white, and they regularly raided British lines of communication between Natal and Pretoria, the capital town of the Transvaal Republic that had been annexed by Britain only the year before, in 1877. With this annexation, the British inherited not only the Boers' long-standing border disputes with the Zulu kingdom, but also the legacy of conflict and bitterness between the Boers and the Pedi nation. This had come to a head following a minor dispute between the Boers and Pedi raiders in early 1876, when the Boer Volksraad (government) unwisely declared war against King Sekhukhune.

On 13 July of that year, the Boers commenced full-scale military operations by advancing on Sekhukhuneland with a force of some 2,000 men led by President Burgers, with several thousand revenge-seeking Swazi warriors in support, determined to defeat Sekhukhune, their traditional enemy fond of widespread marauding. They chose to attack along the course of the Olifants River towards the first rebel stronghold, but, after a chaotic two-day operation, their morale had begun to crumble even before they reached the first Pedi stronghold. The Boer commandos had been reinforced by 2,500 neighbouring Swazi allies, and it was they who bore the brunt of any skirmishing. The Boers then attempted to advance further towards Sekhukhune's main stronghold, but seeing the Boers were battle shy, the Swazis abandoned the campaign in disgust. Boer morale collapsed and their motley invading force retreated, leaving Sekhukhune unscathed and free to continue his marauding.

COLONEL ROWLAND'S ROUTE FROM TRANSVAAL TO ATTACK SEKHUKHUNELAND, 3 OCTOBER 1878

1. Two years earlier, in July 1876, the Boers had been defeated by King Sekhukhune and his Pedi people at Magnet Heights.

N

Zoutspanberg Mountains

2. In 1877 Sekhukhuneland had been annexed as part of the Transvaal by Britain – but the Pedi had ignored this.

Oliphant's River

Fort Oliphant

Steelpoort River

5. During advance British constantly attacked by Pedi in hit and run raids. Rowlands ordered to 'get on with attack on Tatse'.

3. April 1878 Britain sent troops to defeat Sekukhuni under Col. Rowlands VC. It was a puny force of 500 men and only two 7-pound guns.

6. 5th October. Pedi attacked British at night and drove off their horses and cattle, horses later recovered but left Rowland's force ineffective.

Sekhukhune Town.

4. Countryside parched dry after two-year drought. No water or grass for feeding horses or cattle leaving Rowland's force weakened.

Tatse.

8. To prevent Pedi interfering with Chelmsford's line of communication with Pretoria, three forts were built to deter the Pedi raiders but were ineffectual.

7. 6th October 1878 British force so demoralized they withdrew to Fort Burgers.

9. Rowlands' chaotic advance and withdrawal encouraged Zulus to make a determined stand against the marauding British invasion of Zululand.

Fort Burgers

To Pretoria 20 miles.

Fort Webber ◄— 5 miles —►

Magnet Heights

To Lydenburg 80 miles

Mountains

A peace treaty between the Boers and Sekhukhune was agreed at the end of 1876, but the Boer campaign was a military and political disaster for their floundering republic and was one of the factors used by the British to justify their intervention and annexation of the bankrupt Transvaal in April 1877. Seizing the opportunity, Britain annexed the Boer Transvaal, which included Sekhukhuneland. King Sekhukhune never accepted this demarcation of boundaries and subsequent British attempts to establish authority over the Pedi by negotiation were likewise firmly rejected by him. He was now in a state of rebellion against anyone white and regularly interfering with British lines of communication between Natal and Pretoria, then the fledgling capital of the Transvaal Republic.

The beginning of 1878 saw British troops moving towards Sekhukhuneland to finally neutralize the Pedi and to pacify and protect the Boers – now British subjects and clambering for British protection from Pedi raiders. The British despatched Captain Clarke to subdue Sekhukhune, but Clarke's force, equally ill-prepared, was also routed by a combination of Pedi snipers, the ferocious heat and a lengthy drought. They barely escaped with their lives to the safety of the nearby Magnet Heights.

With the British invasion of Zululand imminent, the British commander, Chelmsford, did not want a rebellious Pedi army actively operating behind his northern supply lines into Zululand, and, in August 1878, despatched Colonel Rowlands VC with a fully equipped force of 1,800 men to finally subdue Sekhukhune. Rowland's numbers were absurdly small, especially given the recent Pedi successes over the Boers – no more than a few companies of British regulars were available, along with a handful of locally raised irregular units. After several months of sporadic skirmishes around obscure British outposts, Rowlands was finally ordered to 'get on with the job', to resolve matters once and for all and attack Sekhukhune's capital, Tsate, in the Leolu Mountains.

Rowlands assembled his force at a point about 25 miles east of Tsate at Fort Burghers, and on 3 October 1878, advanced with a force of just 130 men of the 1st Battalion, 13th (Prince Albert's) Somerset Light Infantry, 338 men of the Frontier Light Horse (FLH) and two light 7-pounder Krupp guns. It was autumn, and the country was dry and parched after several years of below-average rainfall. Rowlands advanced just a few miles each day under harassing sniper fire from the Pedi warriors under cover from their familiar rocky terrain, or attacking his bivouacs at night. By the evening of 5 October, he was still several miles short of his objective and his horses were suffering terribly from the lack of water and grass. That night, the camp was again attacked from three sides, and the Pedi managed to stampede the column's slaughter oxen. The attack was driven off after about half an hour but the cattle were lost. The following morning, Rowlands adopted the earlier Boer tactic; he gave up the advance and ordered the retreat to Fort Burghers, which he reached on 7 October 1878.

The British expedition to quell the Pedi had proved only marginally less ignominious than the Boers' attempt, but Chelmsford's accelerating plans for the conquest of Zululand made it impractical to resume any fresh operations against the Pedi. A series of British controlled forts were built strategically around Sekhukhuneland with the intention of containing Pedi counter-attacks, and, from these, sporadic skirmishing would continue up to the end of the year.

King Sekhukhune, who fought against the British in 1878. (*Photo courtesy of Ian Knight*)

By January 1879, few outside Frere's immediate circle of officials knew of the ill-fated Pedi campaign and its ignominious results to date. This was fortuitous, as Britain stood at a high point in its history and enjoyed a second-to-none position in world affairs. Britain was, or so she thought, the greatest power in the world and competently commanded a fine Empire. The British Army was not in the practice of shirking a battle, and not since Waterloo had any power contested her right to rule as and where she chose. However, emboldened by King Sekhukhune and the Pedi people, King Cetshwayo and his Zulu nation defiantly stood their ground when Britain was committed by Frere and Chelmsford to invade Zululand just a few weeks later in January 1879.

The home government in London knew nothing of the failed British attempt to defeat King Sekhukhune or of the pending invasion of Zululand.

Chapter 2

Locations and Invasion Orders
to Column Commanders

Between 6 and 11 December 1879, three large columns of well-trained and seasoned British troops invaded Zululand, the small independent country in Southern Africa, whose autocratic leader, King Cetshwayo, had hitherto been friendly towards Britain. In terms of the proposed invasion of Zululand, General Chelmsford's main invasion force was remarkably small when considering the magnitude of the undertaking. The force of regular troops was initially divided between four main columns, amounting to a total of nearly 6,000 highly professional and well-armed soldiers, and consisted of No.1 Coastal Column supported by the 90th Regiment of Colonel Pearson VC. No.2 Column consisted of 500 well trained Natal Native Horse and one rocket battery under Colonel Durnford; its role was to guard the Middle Drift to block Zulu access from the south into Natal. Attached to this column were some 1,000 locally raised native troops, known disparagingly as the 'untrained untrainables', who were divided into seven battalions and led by recently engaged European officers and non-commissioned officers (NCOs), not necessarily with any military training or command of the English or native languages.

The most powerful No.3 Centre Column consisted of the two battalions of the 24th (The 2nd Warwickshire) Regiment, commanded by Colonel Glyn. Colonel Wood VC commanded the No.4 Northern Column with single battalions of the 2/3rd and 1/13th regiments. A battalion of the 80th Regiment, the 5th Column under Colonel Rowlands VC, was held in reserve at Luneburg in the Transvaal to watch the increasingly belligerent Boers.

All units were supported by detachments of the Royal Engineers, Royal Artillery and irregular units based on the quasi-military Natal Police, together with frontier guards and local defence groups with grand names such as the Natal Hussars, Natal Carbineers and Durban Rangers.

The main invasion's No.3 Column, consisted of some 4,700 men, led personally by the British military commander in South Africa, Lord Chelmsford, an

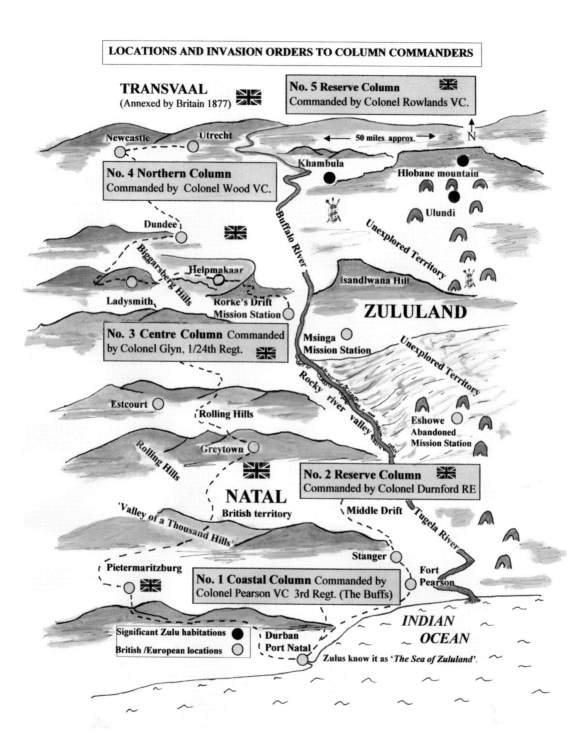

LOCATIONS AND INVASION ORDERS TO COLUMN COMMANDERS

TRANSVAAL
(Annexed by Britain 1877)

No. 5 Reserve Column
Commanded by Colonel Rowlands VC.

Newcastle   Utrecht   ← 50 miles approx. → N

No. 4 Northern Column
Commanded by Colonel Wood VC.

Khambula   Hlobane mountain

Dundee   Ulundi

Biggarsberg Hills   Helpmakaar   Unexplored Territory

Ladysmith   Rorke's Drift Mission Station   Isandlwana Hill

ZULULAND

No. 3 Centre Column Commanded
by Colonel Glyn, 1/24th Regt.

Msinga Mission Station   Unexplored Territory

Estcourt   Rolling Hills   Eshowe
Abandoned
Mission Station

Rolling Hills   Greytown

No. 2 Reserve Column
Commanded by Colonel Durnford RE

NATAL
British territory   Middle Drift   Tugela River

'Valley of a Thousand Hills'   Stanger   Fort Pearson

Pietermaritzburg   No. 1 Coastal Column Commanded by
Colonel Pearson VC 3rd Regt. (The Buffs)

INDIAN
OCEAN

Significant Zulu habitations ●   Durban
British /European locations ○   Port Natal

Zulus know it as 'The Sea of Zululand'.

BRITISH INVASION ROUTES INTO ZULULAND

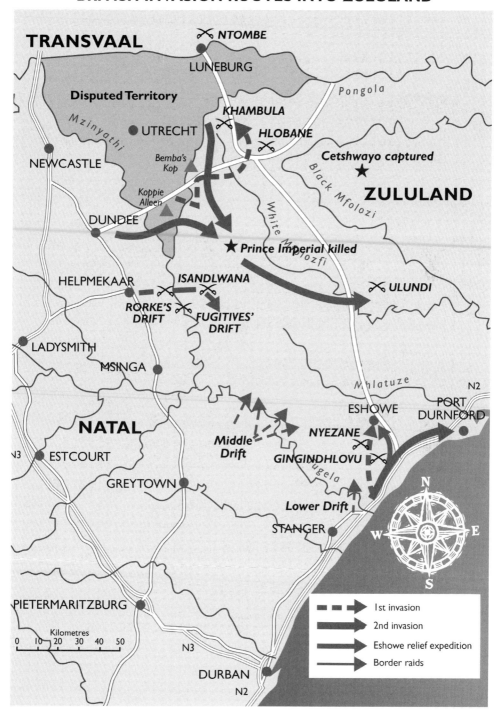

TRANSVAAL

⚔ NTOMBE

LUNEBURG

Disputed Territory

Mzinyathi

Pongola

● UTRECHT

KHAMBULA ⚔

HLOBANE ⚔

Cetshwayo captured ★

Black Mfolozi

ZULULAND

NEWCASTLE ●

Bemba's Kop ▲

Koppie Alleen ▲

DUNDEE ●

White Mfolozi

★ Prince Imperial killed

HELPMEKAAR ●

ISANDLWANA ⚔

⚔ ULUNDI

RORKE'S DRIFT ⚔

FUGITIVES' DRIFT

LADYSMITH ●

MSINGA ●

Mhlatuze

N2

ESHOWE

PORT DURNFORD ●

NATAL

N3 ● ESTCOURT

Middle Drift

NYEZANE ⚔

GINGINDHLOVU ⚔

Tugela

GREYTOWN ●

Lower Drift

STANGER ●

N

W ✶ E

S

PIETERMARITZBURG ●

Kilometres
0 10 20 30 40 50

N3

▪▪▶	1st invasion
══▶	2nd invasion
▶	Eshowe relief expedition
▶	Border raids

DURBAN
N2

experienced and seasoned general with recent experience fighting local native insurrections in the Cape region. His invasion force was made up of the finest British units in South Africa, equipped with the latest Martini-Henry rifles and supported by modern artillery. The invasion was expected to be swift and simple. After all, Chelmsford's force was battle-hardened and rated among the best in the British Empire, while the Zulu army was armed with nothing more than ancient muskets and their traditional knobkerrie clubs and stabbing spears.

Accordingly, the invasion of Zululand was intended as little more than an adventure, with the aim of enhancing the reputations of the soon-to-retire British High Commissioner in South Africa, Sir Bartle Frere, and Frere's military commander, General Lord Chelmsford, a favourite of Queen Victoria. There can be little doubt that Chelmsford and his invasion columns fully expected an early and easy victory over the Zulus. Generally speaking, South Africa was either hot or wet rough fighting country; regardless of hostile conditions, both the infantry and mounted troops would normally engage the enemy by volley fire and then the mounted troops would attack once the enemy was put to rout. Chelmsford knew that in the unlikely event that the Zulus would appear in any number, the British would rapidly form a square or entrench their position to draw the Zulus into the range of their overwhelming firepower. In Chelmsford's considerable experience, well-aimed rifle volley fire from calm and experienced troops supported by rockets, artillery and Gatling guns would, he openly declared, ensure the swift defeat of the Zulu army. It was the accepted policy on both sides that prisoners were not taken; this would shortly be evidenced by the killing of several hundred captured or injured Zulus following Rorke's Drift and then the customary mass killing by cavalry of fleeing and wounded Zulus following successful engagements.

Chelmsford's only fear was that his campaign would deteriorate into a series of 'hit and run' skirmishes similar to those he had experienced in the recent Eastern Cape Colony Frontier War against the Xhosa. He expressed his fear in a private letter 'that the Zulus would not stand and fight':

> All the reports which reach me tend to show that the Zulus intend, if possible, to make raids into Natal when the several columns move forward. The strength of the three columns, Nos. 1, 3, and 4 is only just sufficient to enable them to advance.[1]

---

1. Quoted in *Field Guide to the War in Zululand and the Defence of Natal 1879*, Laband and Thompson, University of KwaZulu-Natal Press.

Chelmsford accordingly devised a three-pronged invasion that would advance on the Zulu capital at Ulundi regardless of Zulu tactics, with each 'prong' or column strong enough to engage and defeat the Zulu army – if it ever stood to fight. The actual tactic was remarkably similar to the Zulu tactic of the 'horns of the bull', and the irony of its use by the British would not have escaped King Cetshwayo and his advisors.

Chelmsford had originally intended that five columns would converge on Cetshwayo's capital at Ulundi but later modified his plan to just three, the Coastal, Centre and Northern Columns. On 8 January Chelmsford wrote:

> Sirhayo [*sic*] has about 8,000 men ready to oppose the crossing. I hope it may be true.[2]

Enthused with their general's optimism, the main British force crossed the Buffalo River into Zululand on 11 January. Although Colonel Wood's Northern Column 'jumped the gun' by advancing on 6 January, everyone's fervent hope was that the Zulus would stand and fight. The first engagement against the Zulus would take place at Sihayo's homestead in sight of Rorke's Drift the following day, on 12 January, just 5 miles into Zululand.

Chelmsford's orders

The Swedish mission station of Reverend Otto Witt at Rorke's Drift was situated on the Natal bank of the Buffalo River border with Zululand and was the only safe crossing point into Zululand for hunters and itinerant traders plying their wares among the Zulus. Sited on an elevated ledge of rock the station commanded a magnificent view across the river into Zululand. Its two small mission buildings consisted of the missionary's house next to a store that doubled as a church on Sundays. Both buildings were solidly made of local stone with thatched roofs. Sheltering the mission was the nearby 700ft high Oskarsberg Hill, named by Witt in acknowledgement of his Swedish king. Surrounding the homestead were 3 acres of carefully cultivated land that included an orchard of grape vines, orange, apricot, apple, peach, fig,

_____

2. Army Records Society, letter to Colonel Wood VC. Perhaps Chelmsford remembered the words of King George III who once observed, 'I am of the opinion that when once those rebels have felt a sharp blow, they will submit', King George III to the Earl of Sandwich, 1 July 1775.

pomegranate and other fruit trees, all bordered by an assortment of lime trees and quince bushes.

Between the vegetable garden and the mission was a 130ft long, 5ft high, stone wall. Witt's home was the larger of the two buildings and was nearly 30 yards long and spacious. Forty yards away was Witt's small and dignified store-cum-church. It was used by the missionary in his daily work with the local black community. Immediately beyond the church was a small stone cattle kraal and then, below the flat rock terrace on which the buildings nestled, there was a similar but larger cattle kraal, that could hold 100 cattle. The sole link between the mission station and the rest of Natal was a rough dirt track that led westwards towards the high escarpment of the Biggarsberg and thence to the small settlement at Helpmakaar. In the other direction, the infrequently used traders' track led to the nearby Buffalo River and into Zululand.

During 9 January the tranquillity of Rorke's Drift was severely disturbed by the arrival of 6,000 troops marching to stirring military music and all the impedimenta of Chelmsford's invasion force. Row upon row of white canvas bell tents were erected in neat formations on the half-mile grassy slope between the riverbank and the mission station, while the Natal Native Contingent (NNC) were instructed to camp downstream of the Europeans. A few days earlier, *The Natal Witness* reported British confidence at a high level.

> No attempt to cross the river will be made if opposed, except under the protection of the battery. These Zulus do not yet know what a shell is like or what effect it will have upon them. May they soon learn, and the larger the quantity that is present the better the effect will be.

The commissary staff under Commissary Dalton commandeered Witt's two buildings on behalf of the Crown and set about fortifying them. In despair at the damage caused by converting his home and church, Witt dispatched his wife and small children to stay with friends at nearby Msinga, some 10 miles south of Helpmakaar. Seeing the magnitude of the British arrival, Witt then set off to follow his family, leaving behind his recently arrived visitor, a young Swedish family friend, August Hammar, to protect his interests. Hammar spoke no English and was understandably presumed by the arriving British to be Otto Witt – a presumption that has confused many subsequent *Rorke's Drift* authors. Hammar was relegated to a small tent near the house. By the day of the invasion, Witt's house was converted into a makeshift hospital to cater for the growing number of fever cases and a few soldiers with damaged limbs caused by wagon-related incidents, while the spare building became an ammunition store. By 11 January, both buildings were fortified, an important fact later admitted by Chelmsford and confirmed by Lieutenant Harford, on loan to the NNC from the 99th Regiment.

Chelmsford arrived at Rorke's Drift during the evening of 10 January with his entourage of staff officers, a visible sign to the awaiting troops that the invasion would take place the following morning. During the night, the six guns of N Battery of the Royal Artillery, commanded by Lieutenant Colonel Harness, were relocated to an adjacent small rise overlooking the river in order to cover the troops while crossing. Shortly after 2.00 am, reveille was sounded, and within the hour the column approached the river crossing point. By daybreak, the river was covered in a heavy soaking mist. No sound could be heard, and as the mist gradually lifted above the river, the far bank and surrounding countryside were bathed in bright sunshine. Contrary to all Chelmsford's expectations, there were no Zulus; they were already 60 miles away at Ulundi, undergoing pre-battle rituals in preparation for the defence of their country.

Chelmsford's Orders to his Commanders for the Invasion of Zululand

No.1 Column: Colonel Pearson VC
Route: Durban, Stanger to Fort Pearson on Tugela River.
Orders:

> Cross the Tugela at Fort Pearson and encamp on the Zulu side; when ordered to advance, to move on to Eshowe, and there, or in its neighbourhood, to form a depot, well entrenched.

No.2 Column: Colonel Durnford, Royal Enginneers
Route: Durban, Pietermaritzburg, Greytown to Middle Drift on Tugela River.
Orders:

> To form a portion of No.1 Column, but act separately, reporting to Colonel Pearson; remaining on the middle Tugela frontier until an advance is ordered, and Colonel Pearson has reached Eshowe.

No.3 Column: Colonel Glyn 1/24th
Route: 120 miles east Durban, Pietermaritzburg, Ladysmith, Dundee to Tugela River.
Orders:

No.3 Column to cross at Rorke's Drift when the thirty days expired; to move forward and form an advanced depot, strongly entrenched, as found advisable from the nature of the country, etc, to assist in clearing the border south-east of Rorke's Drift and keep up communication with the columns on left and right.

No.4 Column: Colonel Wood VC
Route: To advance from Utrecht to Bemba's Kop.
Orders:

To advance to the Blood River. In the event of a further advance, the advance depot of this column to be near the intersection of the roads from Utrecht to Ulundi, and Rorke's Drift to Swaziland; but to delay its advance towards the Umvolosi River until the border is cleared, and to move in a southerly direction towards Colonel Glyn's column to assist it against Sihayo.

No.5 Column: Colonel Rowlands VC
Route: Durban, Pietermaritzburg, Ladysmith, Newcastle, Utrecht to Luneburg.
Orders:

To observe any Boer military activity, whilst maintaining a state of readiness in northern Zululand. (Chelmsford was also concerned that the Pedi army under King Sekhukhune might offer support to the Zulus and create a threat to British supply lines in the north.)

Chapter 3

Helpmakaar to Rorke's Drift,
22 December to 3 January 1879

Route of the main Centre Column: Durban, Pietermaritzburg, Greytown, Msinga, Helpmakaar and Rorke's Drift on the Natal bank of the Buffalo River:

At the time of the Zulu War, Helpmakaar was the main supply depot for Chelmsford's Central Column, through which the whole invading Central Column passed. The name is an Afrikaans word, which translates to 'help one another' in English, and today it consists of an isolated two-man police station, a cluster of mostly deserted and dilapidated buildings alongside the overgrown British cemetery.

The advance of the Centre Column to Helpmakaar was uneventful. Before the invasion there was little at Helpmakaar other than two small rough farmers' cottages and the remains of a tiny church built by a Berlin missionary, Jacob Dohne. To the weary soldiers the location was flat, featureless, remote and bleak. In a letter, Lieutenant Colonel Arthur Harness, who was part of the Royal Artillery's invasion force then at Helpmakaar, described the whole plateau area as devoid of vegetation being 'Like the bottom of the sea with grass on it.' Within days it was a confusing mass of stores and wagons and, due to the summer deluges, there were obnoxious areas of an unhealthy and knee-deep quagmire. Dysentery soon followed. Nevertheless, Chelmsford's force was soon ready to move to the Zulu border.

A considerable area was given over to storage and would have contained several hundred tents and large numbers of horses and oxen. Being flat and level, it was an ideal site for the British to accumulate their vast quantity of supplies for the Central Column prior to the invasion of Zululand. From the top of the Nostrope Pass leading down to Rorke's Drift, the advancing column had a spectacular view of the Buffalo River, which formed the natural border between British Natal and Zululand, and onwards into Zululand with the peak of Isandlwana standing in the distant location.

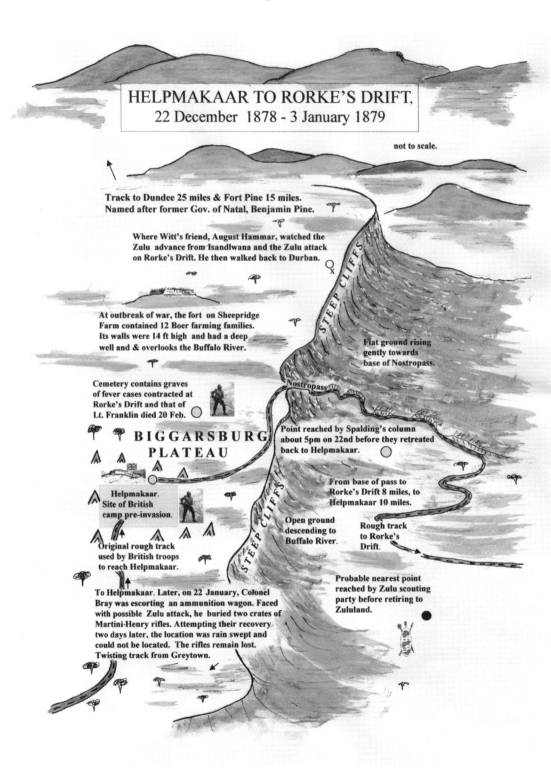

HELPMAKAAR TO RORKE'S DRIFT,
22 December 1878 - 3 January 1879

not to scale.

Track to Dundee 25 miles & Fort Pine 15 miles.
Named after former Gov. of Natal, Benjamin Pine.

Where Witt's friend, August Hammar, watched the
Zulu advance from Isandlwana and the Zulu attack
on Rorke's Drift. He then walked back to Durban.

At outbreak of war, the fort on Sheepridge
Farm contained 12 Boer farming families.
Its walls were 14 ft high and had a deep
well and & overlooks the Buffalo River.

Flat ground rising
gently towards
base of Nostropass.

Cemetery contains graves
of fever cases contracted at
Rorke's Drift and that of
Lt. Franklin died 20 Feb.

STEEP CLIFFS

Nostropass

BIGGARSBURG
PLATEAU

Point reached by Spalding's column
about 5pm on 22nd before they retreated
back to Helpmakaar.

Helpmakaar.
Site of British
camp pre-invasion.

From base of pass to
Rorke's Drift 8 miles, to
Helpmakaar 10 miles.

Open ground
descending to
Buffalo River.

Rough track
to Rorke's
Drift.

STEEP CLIFFS

Original rough track
used by British troops
to reach Helpmakaar.

Probable nearest point
reached by Zulu scouting
party before retiring to
Zululand.

To Helpmakaar. Later, on 22 January, Colonel
Bray was escorting an ammunition wagon. Faced
with possible Zulu attack, he buried two crates of
Martini-Henry rifles. Attempting their recovery
two days later, the location was rain swept and
could not be located. The rifles remain lost.
Twisting track from Greytown.

Having descended from the plateau, Glyn's Central Column waited on the Natal bank of the Buffalo River at Rorke's Drift for the British ultimatum to expire on 11 January. The column consisted of some 4,700 men, 303 wagons and carts and 1,507 oxen. The backbone of this force consisted of both the 1st and 2nd battalions of the 24th (2nd Warwickshire) Regiment. The Royal Artillery had four 7-pounder rifled muzzle loading guns.

Following the battle of Isandlwana just days later, most of the column's survivors escaped to Helpmakaar, which received numerous wounded soldiers. Due to the heavy rains, unhygienic conditions and lack of medical supplies that followed this battle, many of the troops suffered appalling illness and disease. Those who died of their injuries or disease subsequent to these actions on 22 January 1879 are buried in the now neglected and dilapidated cemetery behind the police station. Although anticipated, there was no Zulu attack on Helpmakaar.

Distinguishing features

British cemetery. This cemetery contains the graves of those who died of illness or disease following the events of 22 January. Due to its inaccessibility, the cemetery is usually overgrown and in a state of disrepair. It can be found

British military cemetery at Helpmakaar.

behind the modern police station. Access is by the farm gates either side of the buildings.

1. **Site of Helpmakaar fort.** The outline of the fort can still be seen on the ground.
2. **Nostrope Pass** (along the road to Rorke's Drift but signposted 'Noustroop'). From here one has a spectacular view of the Buffalo River – it was the border between British Natal and Zululand – and into Zululand with the distant and isolated peak of Isandlwana. From this point the British would have had their first view of Zululand and Isandlwana. The Nostrope Pass to Rorke's Drift is a stone/dirt road and descends a very steep hill with a number of severe hairpin bends. In wet weather this route is treacherous and should only be attempted in four-wheel drive vehicles.
3. The original Dutch/Boer spelling of the hamlet was Helpmakaar. The British used Helpmekaar.

Chapter 4

Advance from Rorke's Drift to Isandlwana, 11–12 January 1879

For the advance from Rorke's Drift into Zululand, the backbone of the Centre Column consisted of the two regular battalions of the 24th (The 2nd Warwickshire) Regiment. Both battalions were enthusiastic at the prospect of leading operations against the Zulus. The very experienced 1st Battalion had not seen home service since 1866, when it was posted to Malta before moving to Gibraltar in 1872. They then arrived in South Africa on 4 February 1875, tough and battle-hardened after four years active campaigning during the Ninth Frontier War at the Cape. The 2nd Battalion had arrived in South Africa on 28 February 1878 and shortly afterwards took up duties at King William's Town. Both battalions were then engaged in quelling small pockets of rebellion throughout the Cape area; this added experience helped toughen the regiment in preparation for the invasion of Zululand.

Early on 12 January, the Centre Column commenced the slow advance from Helpmakaar towards Ulundi with the intention of making a supply depot beside a rocky hill then known to the British as *Isandula*; Isandlwana lay about 10 miles from the river crossing and was an ideal site with fresh water and firewood readily available. In between Rorke's Drift and Isandlwana, some 5 miles into Zululand, was a high row of steep red cliffs that formed the backdrop to the homestead of the Zulu Chief, Sihayo kaXongo. Sihayo's homestead lay directly in the path of the invading column's main supply route. Chelmsford ordered that the seemingly empty stronghold be neutralized rather than allow it to sit across his supply line.

It was early on 12 January that Chelmsford and most of his Centre Column formed up to watch the first attack of the invasion against Sihayo's homestead. Colonel Glyn was in overall command of the attack, with Colonel Degacher commanding the 2/24th Regiment in support. Temporarily commanded by Major Black, the NNC was to spearhead the attack, as Commandant Lonsdale was *hors de combat,* suffering from concussion sustained a week earlier when

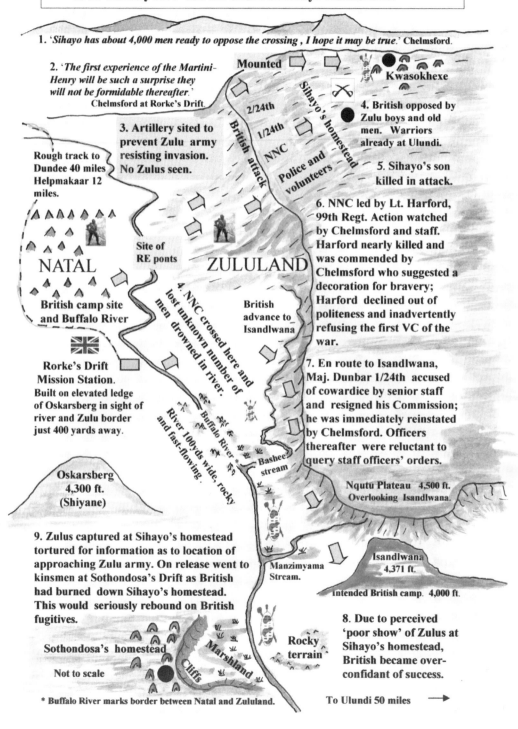

ADVANCE FROM RORKE'S DRIFT TO ISANDLWANA
11-20 January 1879 and the attack on Sihayo's homestead.

1. *'Sihayo has about 4,000 men ready to oppose the crossing , I hope it may be true.'* Chelmsford.

2. *'The first experience of the Martini-Henry will be such a surprise they will not be formidable thereafter.'*
Chelmsford at Rorke's Drift.

Mounted

Kwasokhexe

3. Artillery sited to prevent Zulu army resisting invasion. No Zulus seen.

2/24th

1/24th

British attack

NNC

Police and volunteers

Sihayo's homestead

4. British opposed by Zulu boys and old men. Warriors already at Ulundi.

5. Sihayo's son killed in attack.

Rough track to Dundee 40 miles. Helpmakaar 12 miles.

NATAL

Site of RE ponts

ZULULAND

British advance to Isandlwana

6. NNC led by Lt. Harford, 99th Regt. Action watched by Chelmsford and staff. Harford nearly killed and was commended by Chelmsford who suggested a decoration for bravery; Harford declined out of politeness and inadvertently refusing the first VC of the war.

British camp site and Buffalo River

4. NNC crossed here and lost unknown number of men drowned in river.

7. En route to Isandlwana, Maj. Dunbar 1/24th accused of cowardice by senior staff and resigned his Commission; he was immediately reinstated by Chelmsford. Officers thereafter were reluctant to query staff officers' orders.

Rorke's Drift Mission Station.
Built on elevated ledge of Oskarsberg in sight of river and Zulu border just 400 yards away.

Buffalo River 100yds wide, rocky and fast-flowing.

Bashee stream

Nqutu Plateau 4,500 ft. Overlooking Isandlwana.

Oskarsberg 4,300 ft. (Shiyane)

9. Zulus captured at Sihayo's homestead tortured for information as to location of approaching Zulu army. On release went to kinsmen at Sothondosa's Drift as British had burned down Sihayo's homestead. This would seriously rebound on British fugitives.

Manzimyama Stream.

Isandlwana 4,371 ft.

Intended British camp. 4,000 ft.

Rocky terrain

8. Due to perceived 'poor show' of Zulus at Sihayo's homestead, British became over-confident of success.

Sothondosa's homestead

Marshland

Cliffs

Not to scale

* Buffalo River marks border between Natal and Zululand.

To Ulundi 50 miles →

Sihayo's homestead.

he fell from his horse. The engagement was more farce than action, as Sihayo's warriors had long since departed to join the main Zulu army at Ulundi, leaving only old men and boys to guard their cattle.

Major Black passed responsibility for leading the attack to his young staff officer, Lieutenant Charles Harford, a noted entomologist on loan from the 99th Regiment. This was to be the first engagement of the Centre Column, which sensed some fun to be had from watching Harford in his first action and his 'untrained untrainables' going into action against the Zulus under their equally untrained hotchpotch of colonial NCOs, many of European origin, with little knowledge of English. Led by Harford, the attacking NNC warily advanced towards the steep cliffs and soon came under desultory fire from the homestead's handful of elderly Zulus armed with ancient muskets and old rifles, and boys with sticks. Under their wild and inaccurate fire, the NNC adopted the attack formation rehearsed only the day before and then stormed the stronghold supported by the 2/24th, who ponderously clambered over the rocky terrain several hundred yards to the rear. Peppered by close-range shots from the Zulus' wild firing, the NNC steadily advanced but soon lost half a dozen men killed to random shots, with a similar number badly wounded, while the 24th, who remained well to the rear, sustained no casualties. The defending Zulus, on the other hand, lost over thirty men and boys, killed in one-sided violent hand-to-hand fighting.

Several of Sihayo's old men, including those wounded, were taken prisoner and forcibly interrogated, a rough process that was to rebound on the British a few days later. The captured Zulus nevertheless kept the secret that a great force of 25,000 warriors, accompanied by another 10,000 reserves and camp followers, was steadily closing in on the unsuspecting British. Released the following day, Sihayo's surviving Zulus took comfort at the neighbouring village at Sotondosa's Drift, soon to be known as Fugitives' Drift. Angered by the destruction of their village, the death of one of Sihayo's sons and their own brutal treatment, not to mention the theft of their 413 head of cattle, they and their kinsmen would not be well disposed to the British fugitives who were to flee through Sotondosa's Drift a few days later.

After easily destroying Sihayo's homestead, most of the invasion force moved back to their temporary camp near Rorke's Drift. A detachment of four companies of the 2/24th and some native troops under command of Major W.M. Dunbar of the 24th Regiment were deployed forward in the Batshe Valley between Rorke's Drift and Isandlwana to protect the Royal Engineers repairing the track that ran through two swampy areas leading to Isandlwana. Dunbar was ordered to pitch his tents beneath a rock outcrop close to Sihayo's homestead, in dense thorn with no field of fire. He made his fears known to Chelmsford and asked for permission to move his camp to the other side of the scrub. In the discussion that followed, Chelmsford's senior staff officer, Lieutenant Colonel Crealock, seems to have lost his temper and remarked impatiently, 'if Major Dunbar is afraid to stay there, we could send someone who is not'. Dunbar, a big, imposing man and the regiment's most experienced field officer, walked off in a rage and verbally surrendered his commission, but within the hour he was persuaded by Chelmsford to withdraw his resignation. This incident had serious ramifications, as it deterred experienced junior officers from questioning irrational orders from senior staff officers at Isandlwana.

Over the next two days, local Zulus warned Chelmsford that King Cetshwayo intended to decoy the British and then make for Natal. Chelmsford dismissed their warnings and resolved to push on deeper into Zululand without delay; the low military strength of Sihayo's ill-equipped defenders clearly reinforced his low expectations of the prowess of the main Zulu army, and there would be no reason to fear them.

From the Zulus' perspective, when news of the attack against Sihayo's homestead reached Ulundi, it sufficiently provoked King Cetshwayo and his chiefs to finally order the main Zulu army to advance to attack Chelmsford's Centre Column. Chelmsford's presence during the attack also convinced the king that the Centre Column was the most dangerous of the three and therefore must be attacked first, using the full might of the Zulu army.

Location

The stronghold nestled up against a great blood-red cliff face, beneath which lay a jumble of house-sized boulders. Here, on 12 January 1879, Chelmsford's force, consisting mainly of NNC men supported by the 24th Regiment, easily overwhelmed the near-abandoned homestead as most of the warriors were already at Ulundi preparing for battle.

Note that the road from Rorke's Drift to Isandlwana only approximates the route that Chelmsford took. The old track is still visible from the air, and when the new road was constructed, great care was taken not to damage the old wagon track, which ran from the Manzimyama River onto the saddle of Isandlwana. The new road runs from the Manzimyama River to the north of Isandlwana Mountain.

Chapter 5

The Zulu Army Advance from Ulundi, 16 to 22 January 1879

During September 1878, the British invasion force was ponderously assembling itself at four points along the Zulu border. At the end of the month, King Cetshwayo mobilized his army as a defensive tactic and orders went out to take up arms and 'doctor' or spiritually prepare the army. Three of his regiments, the uMbonambi, uMcijo and iNgobamakhosi, were ordered to report to Ulundi to prepare for manoeuvres along the border. These began immediately and were intended as a serious show of force, and in spite of his army's posturing, Cetshwayo was still desperate to avoid war.

In the final weeks leading up to the British invasion, Cetshwayo had been fully aware that events were rapidly moving beyond his control and ordered wild animal hunts to be held along the border of the territories neighbouring Natal. He sought to ensure that British spies observed the Zulus' advanced state of preparedness as well as the strength of the Zulu army opposing them. Cetshwayo was not to be caught off-guard; shrewdly, he decided to prepare, watch and wait. Aware of the growing consternation of his people at the menacing gathering of British troops along their border, the king sent a number of emissaries to implore British restraint, but on presentation of their credentials they were arrested. In the meantime, the British invasion force continued to mass along the border of Zululand.

Unbeknown to Chelmsford, the timing of his ultimatum to the Zulus worked overwhelmingly in favour of King Cetshwayo, whose whole army was, by coincidence, in the process of assembling at Ulundi for the annual umkhosi, the first fruits ceremony. This was traditionally held each year to allow the king to review his army and herds. Abysmal British intelligence failed to realize that the annual gathering of the whole Zulu army was due to take place just three days before the British invasion of Zululand. Meanwhile, the warriors were instructed to come to Ulundi prepared for war. The gathering Zulu army was soundly structured and consisted of twelve corps, each with one or more

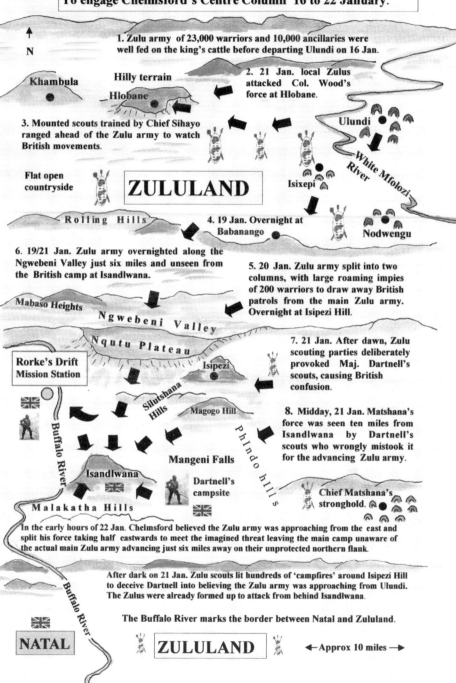

THE ZULU ARMY's ADVANCE FROM ULUNDI.
To engage Chelmsford's Centre Column 16 to 22 January.

N

1. Zulu army of 23,000 warriors and 10,000 ancillaries were well fed on the king's cattle before departing Ulundi on 16 Jan.

Khambula

Hilly terrain

Hlobane

2. 21 Jan. local Zulus attacked Col. Wood's force at Hlobane.

3. Mounted scouts trained by Chief Sihayo ranged ahead of the Zulu army to watch British movements.

Ulundi

Flat open countryside

ZULULAND

Isixepi

White Mfolozi River

Rolling Hills

4. 19 Jan. Overnight at Babanango

Nodwengu

6. 19/21 Jan. Zulu army overnighted along the Ngwebeni Valley just six miles and unseen from the British camp at Isandlwana.

5. 20 Jan. Zulu army split into two columns, with large roaming impies of 200 warriors to draw away British patrols from the main Zulu army. Overnight at Isipezi Hill.

Mabaso Heights

Ngwebeni Valley

Nqutu Plateau

Rorke's Drift Mission Station

Isipezi

7. 21 Jan. After dawn, Zulu scouting parties deliberately provoked Maj. Dartnell's scouts, causing British confusion.

Silutshana Hills

Magogo Hill

Phindo hills

8. Midday, 21 Jan. Matshana's force was seen ten miles from Isandlwana by Dartnell's scouts who wrongly mistook it for the advancing Zulu army.

Buffalo River

Mangeni Falls

Isandlwana

Dartnell's campsite

Chief Matshana's stronghold.

Malakatha Hills

In the early hours of 22 Jan. Chelmsford believed the Zulu army was approaching from the east and split his force taking half eastwards to meet the imagined threat leaving the main camp unaware of the actual main Zulu army advancing just six miles away on their unprotected northern flank.

After dark on 21 Jan. Zulu scouts lit hundreds of 'campfires' around Isipezi Hill to deceive Dartnell into believing the Zulu army was approaching from Ulundi. The Zulus were already formed up to attack from behind Isandlwana.

The Buffalo River marks the border between Natal and Zululand.

Buffalo River

NATAL   **ZULULAND**   ← Approx 10 miles →

regiments with a total of twenty-seven Zulu regiments and more than 25,000 fit and active warriors, ready to take to the field.

On 11 January 1879 the British invaded Zululand, however, in an aggressive show of force, Wood had already provocatively breached the terms of the ultimatum by invading Zululand on the 6 January before the ultimatum expired on 11 January and established his first camp at Bemba's Kop. Wood then rode from Bemba's Kop to meet Chelmsford coming from Rorke's Drift. Wood was additionally requested to protect the Centre Column's flank by neutralizing the Zulus known to be in strength somewhere in the northern Hlobane hill range.

In response to British activity, the Zulu army, totally inexperienced in warfare apart from a handful of veteran chiefs, formed up to receive their orders and undergo purification to reduce the effect of British bullets. Six days later, the army began leaving its base at Ulundi to face the invaders. Their orders were to march directly to Isipezi Hill, then on to a hidden valley behind Isandlwana, 50 miles from Ulundi. A separate *impi* (fighting force) was to engage in a simple but effective decoy to confuse the approaching British before rejoining the Zulu army for their main attack. The army was ordered to march slowly so as to conserve energy. Before they departed Ulundi, the Zulu army was warned that if they lost, they would be shipped to England as slaves and their women and children given to white soldiers.

On 18 January, the Zulu army departed the royal barracks at Nodwengu to pre-determined camp sites at the Isixepi barracks across the White Mfolozi River. They were accompanied by numerous sight-seeing women and children. The army was ordered to 'march slowly' to conserve energy. Although the Zulus could march up to 30 miles in a day, their progress towards Isandlwana was a leisurely 9 miles per day. After dawn on 19 January, the Zulu army split into 2 columns, some 3 miles apart but in sight of each other, with large roaming *impies* of 200 warriors acting as scouts to draw away any British scouting patrols from the main Zulu army. They also foraged for cattle and mealies from local Zulu homesteads. For every four warriors there was an *udibly* youth carrying the warriors' spare equipment and cooking utensils.

On the afternoon of 21 January, from their high vantage point on the overlooking Nqutu Plateau to the north, senior mounted Zulu chiefs were openly able to look down on the extensive British position at Isandlwana. Neither Chelmsford nor his accompanying officers realized the significance of so many mounted Zulus watching the camp, as only senior Zulu chiefs rode horses and no one expressed any curiosity as to what the Zulus were doing.

During the day, Chelmsford received reports suggesting that the Zulu army was approaching his position from the direction of Ulundi. He dispatched a large reconnaissance force under Major Dartnell towards the Mangeni waterfall to ascertain the situation while small groups of Zulus could be seen moving across the hills. Dartnell endeavoured to engage Matyana's skirmishers, who refused to be drawn. After dark, Zulu scouts lit hundreds of 'campfires' around Isipezi Hill to the east of Isandlwana to deceive Dartnell's reconnaissance into believing the Zulu army was approaching directly from Ulundi. Dartnell fell for the trap and immediately requested reinforcements, incorrectly believing he had discovered the Zulu army approaching from the east, whereas the Zulu army was already in its attack position, just 5 miles to the north on the Nqutu Plateau overlooking Isandlwana, but out of sight from the British camp and its patrols. In the early hours of 22 January, Chelmsford reacted by sending half his force – not realizing that the main Zulu Army was already camped to his north-east. The Zulu army silently consolidated its attack formations as Zulu scouts reported the success of their decoy; Chelmsford was dividing his force.

The hidden Ngwebeni Valley from where the Zulu army surprised the British at Isandlwana. (*Adrian Greaves*)

Those remaining in camp settled down for the night, totally unaware that the Zulu army was just 6 miles away on their unprotected northern flank. On the high plateau overlooking the British position, the Zulu forces between the Ngwebeni Valley and along the Nqutu Plateau were ready for their three-pronged mass attack on the unsuspecting British camp. At the same time, Chelmsford's column was arriving at Mangeni in anticipation of engaging the Zulus.

Location

The area of the Mangeni Falls, and its 500ft deep gorge, forms the furthest part of the battlefield of Isandlwana. In 1879, the area, some 12 miles (20km) to the south-east of Isandlwana, was controlled by Chief Matshana KaMondise (Matyana) and included the Hlazakazi and Magogo hills and the Qudeni Bush.

It was while lunching at Mangeni that Chelmsford received the first reports that Isandlwana was under attack, but owing to the fact that the British at Isandlwana did not strike their tents, the distant view through the heat haze suggested that the camp was intact. Chelmsford presumed that, had an attack occurred, the British were in sufficient numbers to win the day easily.

It was only at about 3.00 pm that the unsettled Chelmsford decided to return to Isandlwana to ascertain events for himself. He took with him a small escort and en route he met Commandant Hamilton-Browne, who, having watched the defeat of the camp from a safe distance, tried to persuade Chelmsford that the camp was lost. While the two officers discussed the situation, Commandant Lonsdale rode in from Isandlwana and confirmed the British defeat.

How to find it

After driving from the battlefield at Isandlwana for 12 miles (20km) towards Ulundi, a prominent conical hill to the left of the road becomes very obvious. The road then crosses the stream that leads to the waterfall.

Distinguishing features

Mangani Waterfall and canyon
1. Dartnell's bivouac site on the night of 21 January.
2. The route between Isandlwana and Mangeni is approximately the route taken by Dartnell on the 21 and Chelmsford's force on 22 January.

3. Site of Chelmsford's lunchtime position on 22 January.
4. Site of Chelmsford's proposed camp for the night of 22 January.
5. First hill used by Lieutenant Milne to view Isandlwana.
6. Second hill used by Lieutenant Milne to view Isandlwana.
7. The revised new camp site.
8. Nearby is Hamilton-Browne's ridge, where he observed the Zulu attack on Isandlwana.

Mangeni Falls. (*Adrian Greaves*)

Chapter 6

The First Battle of Hlobane, 21/22 January 1879

Chelmsford had intended Colonel Wood's Northern Column to act as a shield to protect the main invasion column slowly advancing from Rorke's Drift towards Ulundi. Wood had been instructed to advance into northern Zululand as part of a pincer movement in support of Chelmsford's Centre Column and Pearson's Coastal Column to the south, and, at the same time, to engage any local Zulu forces to deter them from joining King Cetshwayo at Ulundi.

Wood had not waited for the expiry of the ultimatum due on 11 January. On 6 January, his column of heavily laden wagons supported by mounted and marching troops had already crossed into Zululand and established a camp near a distinctive hill known as Bemba's Kop. Wood was both impatient and uneasy concerning his scouts' reports of Zulus assembling to the north of his left flank and obtained the general's approval to advance in a north-easterly direction to clear the Ityenka Hill range of Zulus, including the Inhlobane (Hlobane) mountain.

Hlobane is a perfect natural fortress with a 4-mile long level but boulder-strewn summit plateau. It is 1 mile wide, and surrounded by sheer 400ft high cliffs at its upper level, which is penetrated by caves and accessed by a few secret steep paths known only to the local Zulus, the abaQulusi. At the western end, Hlobane was abutted by a lower triangular plateau called Ntendeka and the two levels were connected at the apex of the Ntendeka triangle by a seriously steep and narrow staircase of rocks and boulders just 15ft wide that dropped 200ft from the Hlobane Plateau to the lower Ntendeka Plateau.

Between 15 and 17 January, patrols led by Wood's energetic cavalry commander, Colonel Buller, had pushed along the course of the White Mfolozi River from Bemba's Kop, probing towards Zungwini. On the 18th Buller and his scouts engaged with Zulus around Zungwini but, heavily outnumbered, withdrew to the White Mfolozi River; Buller's report confirmed Wood's impression that the local Zulus were mustering on the Zungwini and Hlobane

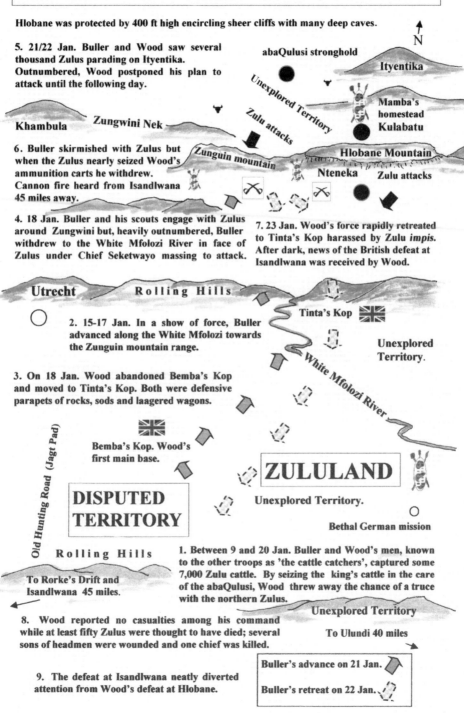

THE FIRST BATTLE OF HLOBANE, 21-22 Jan. 1879

Hlobane was protected by 400 ft high encircling sheer cliffs with many deep caves.

5. 21/22 Jan. Buller and Wood saw several thousand Zulus parading on Ityentika. Outnumbered, Wood postponed his plan to attack until the following day.

abaQulusi stronghold

Unexplored Territory

Zulu attacks

Ityentika

Mamba's homestead
Kulabatu

Khambula   Zungwini Nek

6. Buller skirmished with Zulus but when the Zulus nearly seized Wood's ammunition carts he withdrew. Cannon fire heard from Isandlwana 45 miles away.

Zunguin mountain   Hlobane Mountain

Nteneka   Zulu attacks

4. 18 Jan. Buller and his scouts engage with Zulus around Zungwini but, heavily outnumbered, Buller withdrew to the White Mfolozi River in face of Zulus under Chief Seketwayo massing to attack.

7. 23 Jan. Wood's force rapidly retreated to Tinta's Kop harassed by Zulu *impis*. After dark, news of the British defeat at Isandlwana was received by Wood.

Utrecht   R o l l i n g   H i l l s

Tinta's Kop

2. 15-17 Jan. In a show of force, Buller advanced along the White Mfolozi towards the Zunguin mountain range.

Unexplored Territory.

3. On 18 Jan. Wood abandoned Bemba's Kop and moved to Tinta's Kop. Both were defensive parapets of rocks, sods and laagered wagons.

White Mfolozi River

Bemba's Kop. Wood's first main base.

ZULULAND

Old Hunting Road (Jagt Pad)

DISPUTED TERRITORY

Unexplored Territory.

Bethal German mission

R o l l i n g   H i l l s

To Rorke's Drift and Isandlwana 45 miles.

1. Between 9 and 20 Jan. Buller and Wood's men, known to the other troops as 'the cattle catchers', captured some 7,000 Zulu cattle. By seizing the king's cattle in the care of the abaQulusi, Wood threw away the chance of a truce with the northern Zulus.

Unexplored Territory

8. Wood reported no casualties among his command while at least fifty Zulus were thought to have died; several sons of headmen were wounded and one chief was killed.

To Ulundi 40 miles

9. The defeat at Isandlwana neatly diverted attention from Wood's defeat at Hlobane.

Buller's advance on 21 Jan.

Buller's retreat on 22 Jan.

Location of Buller's skirmish.

hills. During the 21st, Wood and Buller returned to Zungwini to engage the Zulus seen in previous days, inadvertently leaving the baggage and wagons unguarded, and set off towards Ntendeka. Wood then saw some of the Zulus, who had abandoned their positions on Ntendeka, streaming down the hillside and heading unnoticed towards the column's ammunition carts, which had been left with some unarmed buglers. With the Boers and mounted men now disengaging off to his right, Wood sent a hurried message to Buller, whose men intercepted the Zulus before they could sweep down on the column's wagons.

Having skirmished with the retreating Zulus, Buller descended Zungwini at sunset, driving 250 captured cattle and 400 sheep before them back to their camp at Tinta's Kop. Buller's action had lasted for some three hours and, despite a few tense moments, had been an unqualified British success. After dark, Wood and his officers noted the sound of artillery fire way off to the south from, they presumed, the direction of Isandlwana, 45 miles away; Wood commented that gunfire after dark suggested 'an unfavourable situation'. They could all hear Colonel Harness' guns shelling the devastated camp at Isandlwana to clear it of remaining Zulus before Chelmsford re-occupied it after the battle.

On reflection, by mirroring Chelmsford's advance beyond Isandlwana, Wood had similarly intended to take the fight to the enemy by seeking out the Zulus and in so doing had scattered his command over several miles of hilly terrain as he sought to disperse the Zulus. And, like Chelmsford, he had committed the cardinal sin for a military commander in enemy territory of splitting his force and advancing miles away from his base at Fort Tinta – and leaving far fewer men to guard his camp than Chelmsford had at Isandlwana.

Buller's running skirmish with the Zulus would have been considered significant had it not been for Chelmsford's defeat at Isandlwana on the same day. It had the hallmarks of a successful and active engagement and had Wood been able to follow on with further operations led by Buller, the abaQulusi Zulus would, most likely, have been dislodged from Hlobane and scattered. Conversely, when news from Isandlwana reached the Zulus, they were emboldened to strengthen their position on Hlobane. At the time, Buller's men never explored the possibility of finding a route to the vast upper plateau of Hlobane, or any escape route if things went wrong – which suggests a high level of over-confidence on Buller's part for not bothering with such a fundamental reconnaissance. Due to this serious omission, his imminent expedition to capture Hlobane was doomed to failure. In the wake of the defeat at Isandlwana, the first battle of Hlobane was conveniently overlooked by history.

Location

Hlobane is one of the most magnificent of all Zulu battlefields, but it is a notoriously difficult location to visit and an experienced guide, who will obtain the necessary permissions, is absolutely essential for those wishing to reach the flat mountaintop or visit Devil's Pass. It needs a whole day. The fit visitor should be encouraged to climb the eastern end, visit the site of Campbell and Lloyd's graves, and see the site of Buller's ascent and then walk across to Devil's Pass. Beware of sudden thunderstorms.

Take the R69 from Vryheid, travelling eastwards for a distance of 11 miles (18km) in the direction of Louwsburg. After leaving Vryheid, the prominent hill of Zungwini will initially dominate the view to the left (north). Continue along the R69 for about another 4 miles (13km), where Hlobane itself and the prominent Devil's Pass will come into view on the left. The battlefield is situated on the left-hand side of the road, approximately 3 miles (5km) from the road. Take the road to the left signposted to Hlobane. The best view of the mountain can be obtained from this road, which runs through the old coal-mining village and colliery of Hlobane. The road is quiet and there are good photographic opportunities here. To reach the site where Weatherley and his men died, follow the battlefield marker post to the saddle, about 2 miles (3km) from the village. Once on top of the saddle there are spectacular views to the north. Do not proceed further without a guide – the track is a disused mining track and a cul-de-sac of no significance to the battlefield.

Once on top, it is difficult to remain orientated, as there are no obvious landmarks; this makes it virtually impossible to find the way down unless a prominent marker is left clearly displayed near the only exit pathway. Remember that the whole lip of Hlobane consists of sheer cliffs, and there is only one safe way down. The mountain is frequently affected by fog or mist that can cover Hlobane in a matter of minutes. There are also numerous hidden holes across the top, which drop down into caves and underground caverns. Even with a guide, take sufficient water, refreshments and clothing for every weather condition. Good, strong walking boots are also essential due to the very rocky surface on top of Hlobane. Snakes abound.

Chapter 7

Disaster at Isandlwana, 22 January 1879

With roaming scouts on the lookout for British patrols, the Zulu army had marched cautiously from Ulundi to meet the British invaders. King Cetshwayo had ordered his army to 'March slowly, attack at dawn and eat up the red soldiers'. By 20 January, the Zulus had advanced undetected to a point within 10 miles of Chelmsford's column as it ponderously advanced from Rorke's Drift to establish camp at Isandlwana. The unsuspecting Chelmsford, having received intelligence that the Zulu army was within a day's march of the Central Column, and buoyed up by the apparently successful skirmish at Sihayo's homestead, was anxious to engage the Zulus lest they should slip past his force and cross into defenceless Natal. By 21 January most of the supremely confident British invaders had crossed into Zululand and were camped next to a prominent hill, Isandlwana, with unimpeded views for 15 miles towards Ulundi.

The location was ideal. There was plenty of water and wood for cooking, and the position was elevated with a sheer rock face to its rear, making it easy to defend. It looked out east across the open plain in the direction of the Zulu capital at Ulundi so that any approaching Zulu force would be observed for 15 miles before it could attack. The British camp consisted of 750 tents, 1 mile square of neatly erected tents according to strict military regulations. Within hours, the area was transformed into a thriving bustling tent town. Foot patrols were posted to the front of the camp whilst mounted patrols were detailed to the surrounding area, but not onto the Nqutu Plateau overlooking the camp. No preparations were made for a Zulu attack, as Chelmsford had deemed the camp 'temporary'. Having consolidated his position and amassed the supplies needed for his advance further into Zululand, Chelmsford intended to move towards the high ground at iSiphezi some 12 miles on towards Ulundi.

The two armies were now only 6 miles apart, and although the Zulus had a good idea of the British position and movements, Chelmsford refused to believe his scouts' intelligence reports that the Zulu army was steadily

ISANDLWANA   22 January 1879

The Zulu attack and camp defence at noon (final positions).

N

Nqutu plateau 14,500 ft and overlooks the British camp.

NQUTU PLATEAU

Zulu (chiefs) seen here watching camp 7am, seen by Chard about 8 am.

4,500 ft.

Zulu right horn

Magaga 4,478ft.

Noon. Zulu advance controlled from here.

Shepstone, Barton, Raw & Roberts recce group.

12.20 pm Tahelana Ridge 4,202ft. Lt. Dyson's men over-run after firing on Zulu right horn.

Steep cliffs

Shepstone's last stand.

Dead ground

Zulus break through British line

ISANDLWANA 4,371 ft.

C 1/24 F 1/24 A 1/24

Zulu right horn drives in cattle as it advances.

NNC 2/24th RA Mounted	Site of British camp 4,000ft.

RA Guns

NNC

Neither top of Nqutu plateau nor the British front line could be seen from camp HQ due to descending slope.

1/24th

HQ

E 1/24 H 1/24 G 2/24

Lt. Curling failed to save the guns when overwhelmed by Zulus.

BLACK'S KOPPIE 4,150ft.

8. Durnford's last stand.

RA guns wrecked.

Zulus attack Fugitives' route.

7. Durnford's Retreat.

mDlu yengwe

Fugitives' route.

9. Last stand of 24th escapees.

Approx. 1 mile

Zulus disarticulated dead soldiers' beards as trophies. Shaving in the British Army then became popular.

←— Approx. 1/4 mile —→

1. The Main Zulu army advanced about 10—11 am 22 Jan. from the Ngwebeni Valley 5 miles north.

2. 12 Zulu horsemen (chiefs) seen here midday on 21st Jan.

Ithusi Heights 4376 ft.

PLATEAU

Zulu left horn

Nyoni 4,432ft.

Steep ascent to plateau.

Steep cliffs.

Steep cliffs.

umXapho & uMcijo

MAIN ZULU ARMY

3. Russell's rocket battery lost here about 12.45 pm.

uMbonambi & iNgobamakosi

Clear view from British front line of approaching Zulu army.

4. Faced with mass Zulu advance, British outposts retreat back to camp.

uVe

Column's funds and box of gold sovereigns was in care of Paymaster Maj. White. All funds and gold lost when Zulus sacked the camp and never recovered.

Zulu left horn.

NNC

G 2/24

Baking hot at time of Zulu attack. (40°C)

Traders' track to Ulundi (50 miles). →

Conical Koppie 4091 ft. (Lt. Scott's outpost)

6. Durnford's Donga where he delayed Zulu advance.

5. Durnford retreats from mass Zulu advance.

To Rorkes' Drift

At time of Zulu attack at Isandlwana, Chelmsford was unaware of Zulu attack and was lunching at Mangeni Falls (12 miles distant). →

Zulu position pre-attack to the north of Isandlwana.

approaching his position from Ulundi, or that the Zulus were close. He was, however, worried about a line of hills in the opposite direction, Malakatha and Hlazakazi, which shut off his view to the east of Isandlwana. He dispatched a large reconnaissance party under Major Dartnell to the Mangeni Falls adjacent to iSiphezi to investigate the accuracy of the reports. Later that day, Dartnell saw numerous Zulu scouting parties appearing from the direction of Ulundi, and between the Mangeni gorge and the far end of the hill range, a British patrol indeed observed a Zulu force. These were the followers of a local chief, not yet part of the approaching Zulu army.

After dark the Zulu decoy *impi* lit hundreds of fires which patrols interpreted as camp fires of the approaching Zulu army. News of their presence reached Chelmsford just after midnight on 22 January. The message confirmed a strong Zulu force had been seen, and, more importantly, Zulus captured earlier that day confirmed the imminent arrival of the Zulu army, but it was a brilliant Zulu deception, and, after dark, Dartnell observed countless Zulu cooking fires (all decoys) across the hills and reported this to Chelmsford, who mistakenly believed that Dartnell had found the approaching Zulu army.

Chelmsford then split his invasion force with the intention to meet up with and support Dartnell to engage the main Zulu army, and at 3.00 am he departed with a force of 2,500 men, leaving 1,500 men and two guns behind in camp 'in case the enemy should have the temerity to attack the camp during my absence'. Chelmsford's arrogance gave the Zulus an opportunity they could not miss; he had sprung the deadly Zulu trap and placed himself and his senior officers 12 miles away, looking for the Zulus in the wrong direction.

Isandlwana camp was now under the command of Lieutenant Colonel Pulleine, who had never heard a shot fired in anger, with five companies of the 1st Battalion, 24th (2nd Warwickshire) Regiment, one company of the 2nd Battalion, 24th (2nd Warwickshire) Regiment, two guns of the Royal Artillery and some 600 members of the NNC, a total force of over 1,500 men. Pulleine's orders were confusing; he had to defend the position, but at the same time he was to expect an order to move to the next campsite at Mangeni. Isandlwana was unprepared for action in spite of written orders to the contrary, while only 5 miles away behind the Nqutu Plateau, and out of sight of the unsuspecting British camp, the main Zulu army had rested overnight and was now preparing to advance in attack formation.

At the same time, a small column of auxiliary troops under Colonel Durnford, which had been waiting at Rorke's Drift, was moving up to Isandlwana in support of the camp move to Mangeni. Dawn broke as Chelmsford reached the Mangeni gorge just as the Zulus were massing for their attack on his unsuspecting camp at Isandlwana. As dawn broke across Isandlwana, normal camp activities proceeded in a soldierly fashion until the bugle call for breakfast sounded at about 7.00 am. Then things began to go wrong.

The first report came in from a nearby hill that a group of Zulu were watching the camp from the Nqutu Plateau. Then a vague report arrived that a large force of Zulus was advancing towards the camp. The bugler sounded the 'stand to'; breakfast was abandoned, and the soldiers collected themselves to meet the foe, but no Zulus appeared and breakfast was resumed. Then a larger group of Zulus appeared on the nearby plateau, part of the Zulu right horn, and the soldiers quickly responded to the bugle 'stand to'. At about 10.00 am, Colonel Durnford and his column arrived; he expected to find further instructions from Chelmsford, but there were none. Instead, Pulleine confirmed to Durnford the earlier Zulu presence on the high plateau, north of the camp. Rather than remain in camp, and highly suspicious of what the Zulus were doing, Durnford decided to scout the ridge leading to the plateau. He set off at about 11.30 am, and minutes later, his leading riders spotted Zulu foragers driving a small herd of cattle across Mabaso Hill, 2 miles from the camp. They gave chase, but reined in as the ground dipped into a long valley. Below them, sitting quietly and resting, was the leading column of King Cetshwayo's advancing army. Caught by surprise, the leading Zulu regiment rushed to attack, drawing the rest after them.

From the camp, another large mass of Zulus was then seen moving westwards from the camp, so the British ignored them – until the main force came into view from the north, bearing down on the camp from the plateau. A ferocious battle, to be fought to the death of the last British soldier, was about to take place on a hot and dusty African plain. The Zulu warriors were armed with traditional spears and clubs; the British soldiers were equipped with modern rifles and artillery. The 'fall in' call was again sounded for the final time. It was now 12.00 pm and baking hot.

Colonel Pulleine had already ordered his guns and infantry out in extended line to cover the Zulu advance of the left horn to the east of the camp. To the horror of the soldiers, now spread out in a long thin line for 0.5 miles, 6ft between each man, the central body of the main Zulu force, consisting of some 15,000 warriors, appeared to their left and rapidly poured off the plateau, soon to press towards the thin waiting line of British infantry. The two artillery guns commenced firing. Several rounds of shrapnel landed amidst the advancing Zulus, causing some casualties. The Zulus quickly observed the artillery's firing procedure, and, as each gun was fired, they threw themselves to the ground. Most of the shells passed over the Zulu masses and exploded relatively harmlessly, although the charging Zulu regiments began to suffer heavily from British rifle fire. The officers and NCOs in the British front line calmly controlled their men's volleys, and the Zulu main attack stalled. But, to the front of the Zulus, the black smoke from British volley fire had now created a dense wall of thick smoke so that the soldiers could not clearly see their targets. Even so, the soldiers reportedly laughed and joked about the drubbing they were giving the Zulus.

As the Zulu attack developed around him, it was clear to Pulleine that the British position was too extended. Durnford was several miles in front of the camp when he encountered the Zulu left horn, and he was forced to retreat until he made a stand in a deep gulley to the front of the camp. The British position was spread across nearly a mile of open country, and there was a gap of over 400 yards between Durnford and the nearest infantry positions. Despite this, the British fire was very heavy, and for a while the Zulu attack stalled.

Fearing that they could be held at bay, the Zulu commanders, who had taken up a position above a patch of rocks on the face of the iNyoni ridge, sent down an *induna* named Mkhosana kaMvundlana to rally their men. Mkhosana ordered the warriors, who were lying sheltered in *dongas* or among the long grass, to attack. They did, but Mkhosana died in the ensuing fighting.

As the *uKhandempemvu* regiment rose to its feet, all along the line the Zulus surged forward. It was a critical moment in the battle; gaps were beginning to appear in the British line, and Durnford's men were running out of ammunition. As the 'retreat' finally sounded, the Zulus charged through their line – there could be no retreat. The Zulus massing behind Isandlwana now emerged, driving the column's bellowing and terrified cattle through the wagon park and into the undefended rear of the British position. As hand-to-hand fighting raged through the tents and across the foot of the mountain, the British tried to rally on the *nek* below Isandlwana, only to find that the Zulu right horn had already occupied the ground between them and the track to Rorke's Drift. They were trapped.

The scene in camp became one of nightmare proportions, with gunfire, screaming, noise, terror, confusion and slaughter everywhere in sight. The pandemonium was further exaggerated by the bellowing cattle running amok and thick black smoke from the guns spreading across the camp. The fighting and slaughter raged for little more than half an hour before the sheer force of Zulu numbers overwhelmed the remaining soldiers desperately fighting back-to-back.

Most of the soldiers were killed in the violent fighting below the mountain, and the few that managed to escape did so while the Zulu 'horns' were preoccupied with overcoming the last organized resistance. A small group of 24th soldiers attempted a fighting withdrawal to the ravine of the Manzimyama stream, only to be overwhelmed in their turn. By mid-afternoon, only two hours after the Zulus first appeared, British resistance had been wiped out, and the Zulus began looting the camp, carrying away their wounded. The fighting and slaughter had raged for little more than an hour. The Zulus killed the soldiers fighting back-to-back and then their horses, cattle and camp dogs, such was their fury. Whilst no soldier lived to tell the tale, various accounts survive from Zulu warriors interviewed after the battle.

Ah, those red soldiers at Isandlwana, how few they were, and how they fought! They fell like stones – each man in his place.

The soldiers gave a shout and charged down upon us. There was an *Induna* (officer) in front of the soldiers with a long flashing sword, which he whirled round his head as he ran, they killed themselves by running down.

They threw down their guns, when the ammunition was done, and then commenced with their pistols, which they fired as long as their ammunition lasted; and then they formed a line, shoulder to shoulder, and back-to-back, and fought with their knives.

Some covered their faces with their hands, not wishing to see death. Some ran around. Some entered into their tents. Others were indignant; although badly wounded, they died where they stood, at their post.

It did not become apparent to Chelmsford that anything had happened at Isandlwana until late in the afternoon. His command was now scattered and exhausted from trying to catch the elusive Zulus. By the time he managed to march them back to camp, it was dark and the battle was long over. Only the dead, an estimated 1,500 soldiers of Chelmsford's column and 4,000 Zulus, remained spread around Isandlwana.

The Battle of Isandlwana later brought down Disraeli's government and the defeat proved that the British Army was not invincible. For many, it was the first news that Queen Victoria's regiments were even engaged in Southern Africa.

Archaeologists examining British position south of Isandlwana.

Chapter 8

Fugitives' Drift – Formerly Chief Sotondosa's Drift, 22 January 1879

Mid-battle at Isandlwana a gap developed in the encircling Zulu army on both sides of the adjacent Black's Koppie as a group of Zulus broke off to give chase to some civilian fugitives and NNC making for Natal, which was tantalizingly in view from Isandlwana. This temporary gap in the Zulu ranks enabled a small number of the 24th Regiment to follow, only for most to be killed as they were quickly run down by the fleet-of-foot Zulu reserve of 4,500 warriors that joined the chase. It was through this gap that Lieutenant Curling and Major Smith rode alongside the two artillery guns only to see them being driven out of control down the steep, rocky slope behind the camp, where the guns overturned amidst the Zulus who killed the crews. Curling and Smith, both independently mounted, were able to escape the incident and rode on; Smith was killed in sight of the river while Curling escaped.

The main Isandlwana camp fell to the Zulus at about 1.30 pm. The few survivors had already fled round the low rise, Stonie Koppie, which marked the extremity of the camp and made for the rough cattle track leading to the Buffalo River some 8 miles distant. Trooper Westwood of the Imperial Mounted Infantry later wrote, '1.30pm. the Zulus were surrounding us and I and my comrades could do no more, and we had better get away.' An hour later he was saved from drowning in the turbulent Buffalo River by Trooper Wassall, for which Wassall was awarded the Victoria Cross.

The 6-mile route, strewn with rock galleys and boulders, became known as the Fugitives' Trail. Most of the survivors to reach Natal probably did so on horseback, and it can be argued that many of these survivors, with the exception of Curling, Smith-Dorrien, Coghill and Melvill, left Isandlwana some time before the main battle was under way.

As the fleeing NNC and any soldier survivors reached the river, the pursuing Zulus caught and fell upon them. Because the river was in flood, and few of

FUGITIVES' DRIFT (formerly Sotondosa's Drift).
Location of incidents after Isandlwana on 22nd Jan. 1879.

N

Flight of escapees from Isandlwana 6 miles away.

Rocky ground

Manzimyama stream

Fugitives' escape

To Rorke's Drift

Boulder strewn river
100 yards across and in flood.

9. Zulus crossed river and
after taking snuff, advanced
on Rorke's Drift.

Dense bush

1. Last stand of the 24th.

Steep rocky gorge

Steep cliffs

Buffalo River
(Umzinyahti)

Descending high ground

Swamp

ZULULAND

Noxobongo
stream

NATAL

7. Capt. Higginson witnessed
deaths of Coghill & Melvill
then seized Tpr. Barker's
horse and escaped to
Helpmakaar where he was
arrested for desertion.

5. Lt. Smith-
Dorrien jumped
from these cliffs.

NNC fugitives
killed here.

2. Maj. Smith RA
killed here; grave
location now lost.

Flat flood plain

Steep cliffs

Steep cliffs

8. Barker chased up
cliffs by local natives
and escaped.

Sotondosa's Drift

4. Wassel's whirlpool
where he won the VC.

Steep Cliffs

10. Bodies of Coghill, Melvill, Sgt
Cooper and one other found on
1.2.79 and roughly buried. Reburied
by Rev. Smith next day. Coghill &
Melvill later re-interred at present
location.

6. Melvill's
rock

Colour found 3.2.79

3. Many fugitives
drowned in river.

Steep Cliffs

George Bunting's
house and store.

Cooper's cairn.   x

Steep Cliffs

Present day Fugitives'
Drift Lodge.

To Helpmakaar 5 miles.

x   Coghill & Melvill
Cairn and graves.

← Approx. 500 yards. →

the NNC could swim, they tried to make a stand against the Zulus but were quickly overwhelmed and killed. In the midst of this slaughter rode the last of the escapers, some of whom were able to reach the river. An unknown number of other fugitives were killed or drowned in the river under the hail of Zulu gunfire and spears. Curling recalled helping some soldiers to cross the river, letting them hold on to his horse. Having reached the Natal bank, Coghill and Melvill were caught and killed by tribesmen of Chief Gamdana kaXongo, who was sympathetic to the Zulus. These local Natal Zulus, previously indifferent to the British, were ordered by the Zulus harassing the fugitives to join their pursuit – which they did. Other soldiers were similarly caught and killed, including Sergeant Cooper and Private Williams of the 24th Regiment. Captain Higginson escaped and lived to tell the tale, omitting that, having crossed the river, he 'pulled rank' as an adjutant and commandeered a trooper's horse, abandoning its rider to his fate, only to be court-martialled and dismissed. The trooper survived and was later recommended for the Victoria Cross, but the application, by Sir Evelyn Wood VC, was rejected.

For the sixty or so Isandlwana survivors, the first hurdle was to get away from the camp and avoid being hunted down by the Zulus. From the drift, most fugitives fled directly towards the high plateau of the Biggarsberg hills and on to Helpmakaar. The earliest of these escaping riders, rather than risk the wide flooded river, and with the pursuing Zulus not yet evident, instead took a route along the river bank to the first known safe crossing point at Rorke's Drift to alert its defenders.

They then had to cross the turbulent and flooded Buffalo River. Those lucky enough to reach the far bank had to clamber up the steep and rocky hillside and escape into Natal. These survivors mostly made for Helpmakaar, some 12 miles distant. The unlucky escapers were those who reached the Natal bank just before Chief Gamdana's clan learned the British had been defeated at Isandlwana. The following exhausted fugitives, mainly mounted members of the military, then had to face the assegais of the locals still furious at the earlier British attack on their relatives at nearby Sihayo's homestead. There are accounts of some soldiers being swept away in the turbulence of the river, but the number of lives lost in the river is unknown. Also unknown is the location of the graves of others who, having reached the Natal bank, were killed by the Zulus or Chief Gamdana's people. Local folklore relates these bodies were thrown into the river, a local procedure for dealing with the dead.

Sotondosa's Drift (modern Fugitives' Drift).

Previously, Fugitives' Drift, formally Chief Sotondosa's Drift, was an insignificant crossing point, used only by locals when the river was low and fordable. On the 22nd, the river was in full flood – a dangerous raging torrent of water, mud and boulders. Today the route taken from Isandlwana to Fugitives' Drift is well known to local guides and follows a route through the gulleys and rocky ravines until it drops down towards the river.

The first Victoria Cross of the war was awarded for bravery at Fugitives' Drift to Trooper Wassall for saving his drowning colleague, Trooper Westwood, in the river.

Fugitives' Trail Location
From Isandlwana, in the direction of Fugitives' Drift, which can just be seen with the naked eye, the route taken by the battle survivors is littered with whitewashed cairns for a distance of about 1 mile. The first cluster of cairns is clearly visible from the battlefield car park. If venturing down the trail, the services of a guide are essential, as the correct route is boulder strewn and criss-crossed by cattle tracks.

From Fugitives' Drift to Rorke's Drift.

From Fugitives' Drift Lodge, take the track passing the Coghill and Melvill memorial and continue down the hillside to the river. Cross the river and then join the track to Isandlwana. A guide is essential, first to navigate the river and then to follow the correct track. Good walking boots are essential.

Chapter 9

Rorke's Drift, 22 January 1879

This isolated riverside location, linked by a rough track some 30 miles from the nearest hamlet at Dundee, borders Zululand and was originally a quiet trading post, having been established by James Rorke in 1849. He committed suicide in October 1875 having run out of gin. The site was then purchased by the Swedish Missionary Service who appointed Otto Witt as its incumbent.

The drift's battlefield is the most famous of all the Zulu War locations. It is dominated by the Oskarsberg hill, named by Witt after his Swedish king; the Zulus know it as *Shiyane*, the eyebrow. The hill itself abuts the site, which covers a very small area, no larger than the area of two tennis courts, where eight officers and some 130 British and Colonial soldiers held off an estimated attacking force of over 4,500 Zulus for over twelve hours. The core of soldiers involved were from B Company of the 2nd Battalion, 24th (The 2nd Warwickshire) Regiment, whose role was to guard the Central Column's supply base and temporary hospital at the Rorke's Drift insignificant mission station.

During the late morning of 22 January, the recently arrived Lieutenant Chard had returned from Isandlwana where he sought to receive his orders; as these were not forthcoming, he reported back to Major Spalding, the officer commanding Rorke's Drift, adding that Zulus had been seen in the vicinity of the high plateau overlooking Isandlwana. Spalding was aware that two companies of the 2/24th were overdue at the drift from the Helpmakaar camp, some 15 miles distant, so he rode there to ascertain their whereabouts. He left instructions for Chard, the most senior imperial officer present, to take charge.

During the afternoon, a message was brought to the drift that a large Zulu force was approaching the mission station. This was soon confirmed by the few following mounted escapees from Isandlwana, who reported the crushing defeat of the main column. The approaching Zulus had, earlier in the day, constituted the reserve of the Zulu army, which had not taken part in the battle of Isandlwana, some 10 miles from Rorke's Drift. This force then harried the

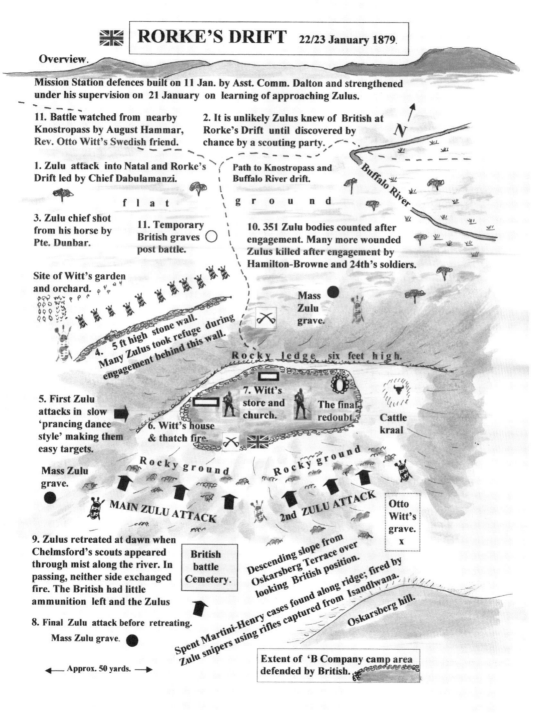

RORKE'S DRIFT   22/23 January 1879.

Overview.

Mission Station defences built on 11 Jan. by Asst. Comm. Dalton and strengthened under his supervision on 21 January on learning of approaching Zulus.

11. Battle watched from nearby Knostropass by August Hammar, Rev. Otto Witt's Swedish friend.

2. It is unlikely Zulus knew of British at Rorke's Drift until discovered by chance by a scouting party.

N

Buffalo River

1. Zulu attack into Natal and Rorke's Drift led by Chief Dabulamanzi.

Path to Knostropass and Buffalo River drift.

f l a t   g r o u n d

3. Zulu chief shot from his horse by Pte. Dunbar.

11. Temporary British graves post battle.

10. 351 Zulu bodies counted after engagement. Many more wounded Zulus killed after engagement by Hamilton-Browne and 24th's soldiers.

Site of Witt's garden and orchard.

4. 5 ft high stone wall. Many Zulus took refuge during engagement behind this wall.

Mass Zulu grave.

R o c k y   l e d g e   six feet high.

5. First Zulu attacks in slow 'prancing dance style' making them easy targets.

7. Witt's store and church.

6. Witt's house & thatch fire.

The final redoubt.

Cattle kraal

Mass Zulu grave.

R o c k y   g r o u n d   R o c k y   g r o u n d

MAIN ZULU ATTACK   2nd ZULU ATTACK

Otto Witt's grave.
x

9. Zulus retreated at dawn when Chelmsford's scouts appeared through mist along the river. In passing, neither side exchanged fire. The British had little ammunition left and the Zulus

British battle Cemetery.

Descending slope from Oskarsberg Terrace over looking British position.

Spent Martini-Henry cases found along ridge; fired by Zulu snipers using rifles captured from Isandlwana.

Oskarsberg hill.

8. Final Zulu attack before retreating.

Mass Zulu grave.

Extent of 'B Company camp area defended by British.

◄— Approx. 50 yards. —►

The view of Rorke's Drift from Oskarsberg hill.

Isandlwana fugitives all the way to the river border before splitting up and approaching Rorke's Drift and neighbouring farms in search of food.

Chard, who was marginally senior to his deputy, Lieutenant Bromhead of the 24th Regiment, realized that with some thirty injured or sick soldiers in Witt's house – now the hospital – they could not realistically outrun the Zulus or escape before they arrived. Assisted by Commissary Dalton, the small garrison began to add to the earlier defences by stacking heavy sacks of mealie corn and biscuit boxes around the position. Helping them were 300 natives under the command of Captain Stevenson, but when the Zulus appeared, this officer fled along with his NCOs and workforce. One of the fleeing NCOs, Corporal Anderson, was shot in the back by a 24th defender; Anderson is buried in the cemetery along with the other soldiers killed in the action.

The defenders were now reduced to 139 men, including the Reverend Smith and Surgeon Reynolds with his 35 patients. During the afternoon, a message was brought to the drift that the Zulus were approaching the mission station. They appeared in force about 4.00 pm and began testing the defences by repeatedly attacking in waves of warriors until after dark – then the hospital's thatched roof caught fire, probably when an army kerosene lamp tipped over. During the following hours, the soldiers occupying the hospital were forced to retreat, room by room, through the building until they reached the high window nearest and facing the British position just 20 yards away. Under constant wild firing from the Zulus, the wounded were lowered one-by-one to the ground; Corporal Allen and Private Hitch, both already wounded, nevertheless successfully ferried the wounded to safety. The hospital was then abandoned to the Zulus.

Whatever the cause of the thatch fire, the blaze inadvertently illuminated the area for the defenders, who were then better able to see and keep the Zulus at bay. By dawn, the British had fired 20,000 Martini-Henry rounds and had just one box of rounds left; they now resorted to repelling the final hand-to-hand assaults with the bayonet, but the Zulus were too exhausted to fight on; when they saw Chelmsford's force approaching the drift, they abandoned the fight and made for the river crossing, which was fortuitous for both sides. In passing, neither the Zulus nor Chelmsford's equally exhausted column survivors exchanged fire.

The Battle of Rorke's Drift is famous, not only for the ferocious action taken by the defending officers and men, but for the recognition of their bravery by the award of eleven Victoria Crosses, seven of which went to the 24th Regiment, the most ever awarded to one regiment for a single action, together with five Distinguished Conduct Medals.

> The General said we were a brave little garrison, and this showed what a few men could do if they had pluck.
>
> Gunner Howard, Rorke's Drift survivor

The battle was watched from a nearby hillside by August Hammar, Reverend Witt's young Swedish family friend, who had been staying with him. After the event, Hammar then walked to Durban and joined the Baker's Horse regiment. He later fought at Ulundi, after which he became a noted coastal surveyor and undertook, on foot, the first complete survey of the Victoria Falls. It was his later letters to his family that confirmed Rorke's Drift had been prepared for defence several days before the Zulu attack.

> The defeat of the Zulus at this post, and the very heavy loss suffered by them, has, to a great extent, neutralised the effect of the disaster at Isandhlwana, and no doubt saved Natal from a serious invasion.
>
> Lord Chelmsford, 8 February 1879

With the battle over, Chelmsford, Colonel Glyn and their team of staff officers arrived back at the Rorke's Drift mission station and, in theory, resumed command of the shocked and battered garrison, a garrison whose morale had seriously plummeted. This relegated Chard and Bromhead back to their normal regimental duties, and there is no record or account of Chard or Bromhead having any further impact on the scene thereafter; they had performed their duties bravely and admirably. Chelmsford had thanked the assembled defenders and, in the minds of the two officers and all the soldiers involved, some had survived, some had died, and that was that.

The newly combined garrison of the Rorke's Drift defenders, and Chelmsford's recently arrived force was now in a state of chaos, distress, exhaustion and confusion; every man had either fought for twelve hours in the defence of Rorke's Drift or had been part of Chelmsford's force that had, in intense heat, marched 50 miles in the previous forty-eight hours and witnessed the results of the slaughter of their colleagues at Isandlwana. The fierce heat of the previous two days had now given way to torrential rainstorms, and there were no tents to accommodate the troops. The garrison was without vital supplies, and the troops were terrifyingly low on ammunition; most of the day-to-day stores and essentials had been lost or damaged in the battle, and those stores that had been despatched to Isandlwana were beyond reach, either destroyed or looted by the Zulus.

In the midst of this distressingly desperate situation, there was so much to be done; there were the British dead to be buried and hundreds of Zulu bodies piled up that needed to be cremated. The sick and injured required urgent medical treatment and the remaining stores had to be sorted and unpacked in the attempt to find food for the 700 men. It was to be several days before good military discipline and order was finally restored. Meanwhile, the Zulu army, its location unknown, was still expected to descend upon the mission station without much warning.

After the engagement, 351 Zulu bodies were counted and cremated. Many more wounded and exhausted Zulus were killed in the hours following the Zulu withdrawal by Hamilton-Browne's and Chard's men; bodies away from the camp perimeter were left to the elements. After the Zulus departed, the area around Witt's house and store was re-barricaded for fear of another Zulu attack. During the day, 23 January, Chelmsford's column returned to Rorke's Drift which strengthened the garrison to over 1,000 officers and men, with a similar number at Helpmakaar. Both positions were re-fortified against a further Zulu attack, but the resulting pollution and constant heavy rain soon resulted in widespread sickness. Conditions at Rorke's Drift became so serious that by March, the whole position was moved to an adjacent hilltop overlooking the river and named Fort Melvill. Once it was realized that the threat of a Zulu attack was unlikely, both garrisons were closed down and the troops moved to Dundee in preparation for the second invasion.

Sanitising the Isandlwana disaster

> One of the things that no fellow can understand.
> Lieutenant Colonel Pickard of the Royal Household

As and when the soldiers had any spare time, some sought to write letters home, but all available paper had been burnt in the fire or destroyed during the fighting. When Commandant Hamilton-Browne sought to arrange a field court-martial for a captured Zulu spy, he had great difficulty finding paper or pens to record the proceedings. All of a sudden, paper had become a very rare commodity; one soldier, Private Robert Head, was so desperate to write a letter to his brother with the news that he was still alive that he paid 1 shilling, a day's pay, for a scrap of paper burnt on two sides. This scrap of a letter survived – but the true identity of the soldier remains unknown, as there was no Private Robert Head recorded either in the 24th Regimental records or on the list of Rorke's Drift defenders. Presumably, he wrote home using his correct name, but at the time of his enlistment, he used a false name.

Of greater significance is the statement by Lieutenant George Stanhope Banister of the 2/24th who, having accompanied Chelmsford during the previous four days, found himself appointed as Assistant Garrison Adjutant at Rorke's Drift. In a brief note to his father dated 27 January 1879, Banister wrote, 'No paper or pens or in fact any single thing. I have managed to get some foolscap in my extra capacity as Garrison Adjutant.' Likewise, without paper, no camp orders could be issued until the 28 January, six days after the battle, when a limited official supply arrived from Helpmakaar. The soldiers had to continue to make do with scraps; one soldier, Private John Bainbridge, even sent a note to his family in England with a request for writing paper – on the grounds that there was 'none to be had within 200 miles of here'. Lieutenant Curling, who was a compulsive letter writer, couldn't find any writing paper; he bemoaned his plight but was thankful to have been the sole survivor from the British front line at Isandlwana. He eventually managed to write home and stated:

> One ought not to think of anything after having had such a wonderful escape. As to clothing, blankets etc., there have been sales of all the kits belonging to the officers who were killed, and I have been able to get the most necessary things one requires. This paper I am writing on belonged to one of the poor fellows in the 24th.

Extraordinarily, amidst the incessant heavy downpours of rain, the mire and chaos, and within two days of the battle, Chard somehow managed to obtain a sufficient supply of clean undamaged paper in order to prepare and submit a perfectly sequential report of the battle that was carefully composed, neatly written and complete in surprising detail. The report, apparently written in secret, included precise timings, specific locations and included the names of the thirteen different units represented, as well as listing the names and units of those who were killed, injured or who might receive acknowledgment for their outstanding courage during the battle. Yet, there is no known record of any participant in the battle having assisted Chard with his report, neither is it known how he was able to accurately recall the names of all the participants or draw accurate pictures of the hospital building after it had been destroyed by fire, and more curiously, the whole engagement took place in the dark. Bromhead was subsequently requested to write an account, but he repeatedly avoided the issue until 15 February, when he allegedly wrote a brief report outlining the bravery of certain participants in the battle. Likewise, there is no evidence that any of the NCOs present during the battle assisted Chard or Bromhead in the preparation of their reports. Colour Sergeant Bourne left no contemporary account.

For an officer with a reputation for slothfulness, and given the extraordinarily difficult circumstances under which Chard's report was written, the result is a truly masterful and perceptive account of the battle. Curiously, if Chard made any notes in the preparation of the report, they have never been seen. When, over twelve months later he was asked to re-write the account for Queen Victoria, he reported that he had 'lost' his original notes – if he had written any in the first place.

Although Chelmsford had not remained at Rorke's Drift for more than a few hours, he had given specific instructions for a formal enquiry to be conducted into the Isandlwana defeat; it is also probable that he ordered a report concerning the victory at Rorke's Drift. It is now known from recently discovered letters that Chelmsford knew that an account was being prepared; his own correspondence reveals that he was most anxious to receive the account, although it is not known who ordered it or who was to write it. As early as 28 January, Chelmsford wrote to Glyn:

> I hope you are sending me in a report of the defence of Rorke's Drift post and also the names etc. of the killed during that gallant fight.

On 31 January, Glyn received a further request for his overdue report from Chelmsford's staff officer. This request is ambiguous, as it uses the word 'reports', indicating that Chelmsford was expecting at least two reports, presumably concerning Isandlwana and Rorke's Drift. He wrote;

> Your immediate attention is called to the fact that no reports have been received from you regarding the entrenchment of your column or of the occurrences of the 22nd instant; neither has any return of casualties been made.

On 3 February Glyn received a further curt note from Chelmsford marked 'Private', reminding him that Chelmsford was still waiting for the Rorke's Drift report. Glyn was suffering depression from the loss of his regiment and friends, he had also been warned of rumours that he was to be a scapegoat for Isandlwana – Glyn either ignored or was unable to attend to the communication. His suspicions were soon confirmed when he received a more formal request from Chelmsford's staff for information relating to Isandlwana. Glyn's reply was abrupt and to the point: 'Odd the general asking me to tell him what he knows more than I do.'

In the meantime, Chard's pristine and detailed report somehow found its way to Chelmsford, who immediately forwarded it to the Secretary of State for War. It would have been in Chelmsford's interest to have a dramatic report of the victory at Rorke's Drift, which he could then promulgate. He knew Rorke's Drift had the potential to portray a spectacular victory that would effectively deflect those who would soon seek to humiliate him for the appalling loss of men and the longer-term implications of a highly trained British force being defeated by a native army. Chelmsford's advisors would also have been aware that, especially in the minds of the British press and public, an inglorious defeat could be offset by a glorious victory. And so it was. Furthermore, before Parliament could act to censure Chelmsford for his unexpected and unauthorised invasion of Zululand, Queen Victoria pre-empted any criticism by ordering a congratulatory message to be sent to Chelmsford via the Secretary of State for War:

> The Queen has graciously desired me to say she sympathises most sincerely with you in the dreadful loss which has deprived her of so many gallant officers and men and that Her Majesty places entire confidence in you and in her troops to maintain our honour and our good name.

This was followed by a further message from Field Marshal His Royal Highness The Duke of Cambridge, Commander-in-Chief of the British Army. His telegram reads:

> Have heard, by telegraph, of events occurred. Grieved for 24th and others who have fallen victims. Fullest confidence in regiment, and am satisfied that you have done and will continue to do everything that is right. Strong reinforcements of all arms ordered to embark at once, February 13th.

The Chard Report concerning Rorke's Drift was initially hailed throughout the British and Colonial press as evidence of Britain's strength in adversity, and both Chard and Bromhead were fêted in the newspapers and popular weekly journals as heroes. However, amongst their fellow officers there was a certain amount of growing resentment and incredulity for their unexpected status as popular heroes. Curling and other officers who had been witness to so much on that fateful day were soon annoyed by the intensity of fame being attached to the two officers. Curling, the only officer to survive the front line at Isandlwana, wrote:

> It is very amusing to read the accounts of Chard and Bromhead. They are about the most common-place men in the British Army. Chard is a most insignificant man in appearance and is only about 5 feet 2 or 3 in height. Bromhead is a stupid old fellow, as deaf as a post. Is it not curious how some men are forced into notoriety?

On 15 February, Bromhead submitted his report concerning the bravery of six soldiers of the 24th during the battle of Rorke's Drift. Subsequently known as the 'Bromhead Report', it is short and to the point and was signed by Bromhead and submitted to Glyn, the regiment's commanding officer, who relayed it without any comment to Chelmsford. It is not known who actually prepared or wrote the report, although Bromhead signed it in his capacity as the commander of B Company. Curiously, and highly irregularly, Chelmsford personally added the names of Chard and Bromhead to the report without further comment. Why Chelmsford did not discuss with Glyn the matter of awards for the two officers is not known; Glyn had not seen fit to recommend them, and in accordance with established military protocol, any recommendation should have come from Glyn as the commanding officer of Rorke's Drift.

Apart from the 'Bromhead Report' and his note warning those at Helpmakaar, only two other letters are known to have been written by Bromhead. The first was written to Captain Goodwin-Austen of the 2/24th on 19 February. Goodwin-Austen had been with Chelmsford on the 22/23 January. It can be clearly seen that the style and syntax in the official Bromhead Report differs considerably from that used in the two letters – which indicates that Bromhead was not the author of the official Bromhead Report.

Some authors have long believed that Chard could not have written the first 'Chard' report, it being too accurate and academic for him, and he was not trained to compile such a complex report. The author could have been any erudite officer who had been able to piece together the sequence of events. The most likely candidate has to be Chelmsford's senior staff officer, Major Francis Clery, who had curiously remained behind at Rorke's Drift after Chelmsford and his staff departed on 24 January. Why did he remain? Chard's 'official' report is dated the following day. Clery was a confidant of Chelmsford and an experienced report writer. He was a staff college graduate, a former Professor of Tactics at Sandhurst Military College, very self-assured, observant and prone to making gossipy judgments about his colleagues. Clery had also been culpable in the unfortunate decision-making process that led to the defeat at Isandlwana, and he, of all people, would have realized that a dramatic report from Rorke's Drift might deflect the criticism that would undoubtedly be unleashed upon Chelmsford and his staff.

However, a recent scientific investigation into the Chard Report suggests otherwise. An in-depth review and analysis of handwriting and style was undertaken by Dr David Holmes and his team of The College of New Jersey, USA. Their analysis concluded as follows:

Stylometric analysis of the Chard Report has given us no clear and definite authorship. There remains the possibility that an original report by Chard was passed through several hands, so that multiple corrections, additions, subtractions and stylistic improvements, all contributed to shape the final report, which was then transcribed by a totally different hand. It was very likely that such an important document, with the potential to exonerate the senior officers from blame for Isandlwana by building up the victory at Rorke's Drift, would be reviewed and amended before final submission. No senior officer would pass a report on such an important event until it had been put in the most favourable form. The Chard Report should be viewed in that light, and should be regarded as a compilation of the available facts, which was then signed by Chard. This research project now lies somewhat tantalizingly on hold.

Pulling the strings

Following the victory at Rorke's Drift, the glowing reports of the battle swiftly and effectively distracted public attention away from the ignominious disaster at Isandlwana. However, the heroic accounts of outstanding bravery effectively maintained the reputation of the army and calmed anxious British politicians, press and public alike. To maintain public morale, official recognition, decorations and medals for bravery followed. At first the matter was clear cut: the highest military award, the Victoria Cross, was to be awarded to the six soldiers named in the Bromhead Report. Curiously, the two officers in the forefront of the action, Lieutenants Bromhead and Chard, were included with the names of six soldiers, but only after Chelmsford secretly added the officers' names to the list. This was an unprecedented breach of military protocol, which was further overlooked by the War Office, as neither of the two officers responsible for these medal recommendations were ever consulted, namely Chard, as the senior officer present during the battle, nor Glyn as the overall commander of those involved. Again, Lieutenant Colonel Pickard raised the matter in a letter to Sir Evelyn Wood (commander of the Northern Column in Zululand) after Chard had been to Balmoral to meet Queen Victoria. Pickard wrote on the matter:

It seemed odd to me that he (Chard) was not consulted on the distribution of the VCs. But it is only one of the things that no fellow can understand. He is not a genius, and not quick, but a quiet, plodding, dogged sort of fellow, who will hold his own in most situations in which, as an English officer, his lot may be cast.

Without doubt, the award of so many decorations and medals was due as much to the perceived propaganda value for the government of the victory than a measure of the undoubted bravery of those involved. There can be little doubt that, as author Ian Knight wrote, 'by elevating Rorke's Drift to the level of a major strategic victory, the more damaging significance of Isandlwana was obscured'. This view was first tauntingly and openly aired by Lieutenant General Garnet Wolseley, the new Commander-in-Chief and General Officer Commanding South Africa. He stated that it was:

monstrous making heroes of those who saved or attempted to save their lives by bolting or of those who, shut up in buildings at Rorke's Drift, could not bolt, and fought like rats for their lives, which they could not otherwise save.

Wolseley certainly voiced his criticism of the awards, but it was Wolseley who had personally been obliged to escort Chard and Bromhead's Victoria Cross decorations all the way from London. The timing of the awards was also significant; it can hardly be chance that it coincided to the day with the second invasion of Zululand, when morale throughout the new invasion force was not high, especially among the many troops, largely inexperienced and fresh from England. Those recently landing in South Africa were, after all, in some trepidation at the prospect of meeting the hitherto victorious Zulu army, with its awesome reputation, although the widespread publicity of the award of an unprecedented number of Victoria Crosses would certainly have pleased the troops and boosted their morale.

Meanwhile, Chard and Bromhead were immediately promoted to captain and brevet major; both promotions were backdated to 23 January 1879.

Bromhead became a major on 4 April 1883. Chard was subsequently promoted to major on 17 July 1886.

Understandably, the awards were extremely popular with the British press and their readers and, quick to recognize the mood of the people, the War Office soon considered making further awards, especially as questions were being asked in parliament as to why the ordinary soldiers at Rorke's Drift had not been nominated or considered for their acclaimed acts of bravery. It was also realized by the press that the only known nominations to date were for members of the 24th Regiment. In the House of Commons, a number of difficult questions were asked: some boldly challenged the involvement of Queen Victoria and her uncle, HRH The Duke of Cambridge as Commander-in-Chief of the Army.

On 27 March 1879 MP Mr Osborn Morgan, asked Colonel Stanley as Secretary of State for War why no awards had been conferred upon NCOs and private soldiers. The reply given was that such awards took a considerable time to process – but that the matter was already under consideration. Another MP, Doctor Ward, asked on 8 May why Surgeon Reynolds had been overlooked for an award. The Secretary of State for War gave a defensive reply stating that it was premature for him to consider what awards or honours should be given; he then added that Surgeon Reynolds had already been promoted fourteen months in advance of his seniority and had passed over the heads of sixty-four other medical officers. Nevertheless, the first to benefit from such serious lobbying was Surgeon Reynolds; although his promotion to Surgeon Major was backdated to the date of the battle, his name was subsequently added to the medal list on the 17 June 1879.

Mr Stacpoole MP and other members of parliament maintained pressure on Colonel Stanley when, on 16 June, they scathingly asked whether it was true that, in recognition of the gallantry of the NCOs and privates at Rorke's Drift, they had been awarded one free flannel shirt and one pair of trousers. Colonel Stanley, clearly stung by the innuendo, replied that such an order had been given to compensate the soldiers for damage to their uniforms and lamely added, 'whether regard was had for gallantry or not I cannot say'.

Other reports began to circulate in England and South Africa about Commissary Dalton's role at Rorke's Drift. The belief grew that it was Dalton who was mainly responsible for the successful defence, especially when rumours were confirmed that he had previously gained a military qualification in field fortifications. Questions about Dalton's role were asked both in parliament and by The Duke of Cambridge, so the matter was referred on to Sir Garnet Wolseley, the new Commander-in-Chief and General Officer Commanding South Africa. Wolseley had already written about his unease:

> I presented Major Chard RE with his Victoria Cross, a more uninteresting or more stupid looking fellow I never saw. Wood tells me he is a most useless officer, fit for nothing. I hear in the camp also that the man who worked hardest at Rorke's Drift Post was the Commissariat Officer, who has not been rewarded at all.

Clarification of the matter was finally sought from Major Chard, who was asked to comment on the actions of both Dalton and Dunne. Rather surprisingly, he acknowledged their actions, but his reply was weak and vague. Undaunted, Dunne's and Dalton's Commissary General, Sir Edward Strickland, was convinced that the actions of his officers in the defence of Rorke's Drift had been deliberately overlooked; he wrote to Chelmsford in his new capacity as Military Secretary at the War Office, and within a week the correspondence concerning the matter was placed before The Duke of Cambridge. His decision on the 18 October was short, final, and worse, unfair.

> We are giving the VC very freely I think, but probably Mr Dalton had as good a claim as the others who have got the Cross for Rorke's Drift defence. I don't think there is a case for Mr. Dunne.

Dalton was awarded the Victoria Cross in November 1879, which was presented by Major General H.H. Clifford on a parade at Fort Napier. Rather perversely, Dunne received nothing other than the knowledge that he had been recommended for the VC. Nevertheless, Dunne fared well. He was involved in the first Boer War in 1880–81 and was present at the Battle of Tel-el-Kebir when the British defeated the Egyptian army. He transferred to the newly formed Army Service Corps as a lieutenant colonel, was awarded a CB and retired as a full colonel.

Disquiet had also been voiced by officers with the Colonial forces present during the event because their men had been omitted from the medal list. When this was realized, the reports were re-examined, and on 29 November,

Corporal Schiess of the NNC was gazetted as a recipient of the Victoria Cross for his actions during the battle. When he received his medal from Sir Garnet Wolseley on 3 February 1880, Wolseley expressed the wish that Schiess might live long to wear the decoration. Sadly, he was to die a pauper only three years later.[3]

The allocation of Victoria Crosses for Rorke's Drift was so disjointed that the time-span of awards extended to more than one year, and apart from the intense background politicking and intrigue, each award was given the highest level of publicity by the press, for which the government was equally grateful. Even so, there were dissenters. *The Broad Arrow* of 23 August 1879 wrote:

> It must be confessed that the military authorities in Pall Mall have shown lavish prodigality in the distribution of the Victoria Cross, which would probably startle their contemporaries in Berlin (a reference to the profusion of Iron Cross awards). We say there is a chance of the Victoria Cross being cheapened by a too friendly eagerness in Pall Mall to recognise acts of equivocal valour.

It is a myth that the Reverend George Smith was offered the choice of a Victoria Cross or an Army Chaplaincy; he received the chaplaincy but there is no evidence or recommendation to substantiate the story that he ever had a choice.

Chard continued to enjoy royal favour and rose in rank to colonel. He was posted abroad several times but never saw action again. In 1896, he was diagnosed with cancer of the tongue and forced to retire. Queen Victoria was kept informed of his deteriorating condition, which led to his death in November 1897.

An interesting postscript concerning Chard's Victoria Cross occurred in 1999. Stanley Baker, who played Chard in the celebrated film *Zulu*, acquired Chard's pair of medals at auction in 1972. Although the campaign medal was genuine, the Victoria Cross was catalogued as a copy, and, as a consequence, Baker paid the comparatively modest sum of £2,700 for the pair. On Stanley Baker's death, the VC changed hands three times, until it ended up, lodged for safety, with Spink medal dealers, who decided to check the nature of

---

3. Survivor's account *British Battles*, Cassell 1898.

Chard's 'copy' Victoria Cross. Its metallic characteristics were tested by the Royal Armouries and compared with those of the bronze ingot, kept at the Central Ordnance Depot, from which all Victoria Crosses are cast. The tests revealed that the 'copy' had come from this same block, and there was no doubt that it was the genuine article. No price can be put on this authenticated VC belonging to such a famous recipient.

With the exception of Robert Jones's medal, all the VCs belonging to the men of the 24th are now on display at the The Royal Welsh Regimental Museum at Brecon.

Rorke's Drift landmarks

The Buffalo River. The Buffalo River at Rorke's Drift at the time of the Zulu War constituted the border between Natal and Zululand; its track crossing the river was an old trading route, snaking its way from Rorke's Drift to Ulundi – the route that Chelmsford intended to follow on expiry of the ultimatum. At midnight on 10 January 1879, Chelmsford forded the Buffalo River at Rorke's Drift at the head of the Central Column, made up of 4,709 officers and men, 220 wagons, 82 carts, 49 horses, 67 mules and 1,507 oxen. His objective was the Zulu capital, Ulundi, 65 miles (108km) away to the east.

The 'Old Drift'. The Old Drift is the original river crossing point and the site of the infamous 'Sihayo incident'. About 400 yards downstream from the bridge, the river runs over a series of rock shelves, which constitute the 'old drift', a natural causeway where people and wagons could gain purchase when crossing – hence the importance of the site. In the winter of 1878, Chief Sihayo kaXongo Ngobese of the Qungebe people lived in the Batshe River area opposite Rorke's Drift, where he had two adulterous wives stoned to death at the river crossing. This incident was seized upon by the British High Commissioner, Sir Bartle Frere, and woven into the pre-amble of the British ultimatum. It was made to look like an aggressive Zulu cross-border incident.

The ferry pool, just upstream from the present day low-level bridge was where the British established their ponts. This position is commanded on the Natal (western) side by a ridge, upon which the British built a sandbag and palisade fort called Fort Melvill in honour of the Lieutenant Teignmouth Melvill VC.

This fort was garrisoned after the battle of Rorke's Drift. Downstream from the drift, on the bend in the river, two old pont stanchions marked with the date '1863 Camel steel' still stand today.

Memorial at Rorke's Drift.

Fort Melvill. In April 1879, hygienic conditions at the mission station seriously deteriorated, which led to mass sickness causing the Rorke's Drift garrison to be moved to an adjacent hilltop overlooking the river.

Meij's Hotel. Sometimes referred to as 'May's Hotel, was built as a private venture towards the end of 1879. When it was completed, the British placed it 'out of bounds', and the enterprise failed.

The British Cemetery. Where the Rorke's Drift battle dead are buried. The centre monument was crafted by Private Mellsop of C Company 2/24th; he had been a stonemason by trade before enlisting with the 24th Regiment. All fever cases were buried across the river, downwind, at the second British cemetery.

Second British military cemetery. This site was rediscovered in 1999 by Petros Sibisi and Nicky von der Heyde, who were searching for evidence of the wagon track built between 14 and 20 January 1879, linking Rorke's Drift and Isandlwana. The overgrown cemetery was in the centre of a dense grove of gum trees. The site has since been restored. There are some graves of soldiers, part of the garrison of Fort Melvill, who died of fever. There are also some more recent civilian graves in this cemetery, dating from the Boer War. Nearby are the remains of Fort Northampton, a sandbag or palisade fort built on the Zulu riverbank just after the Anglo-Zulu War, when this region was racked with civil war. Its outline is still discernible, as is the deep well cut into the sandstone.

The church. The store/hospital during the battle.

Zulu graves. There are three marked mass Zulu graves at Rorke's Drift, each with a plaque in English, Zulu and Afrikaans. Other Zulu battlefield memorials are at Isandlwana, Ulundi, Nyzane and Khambula.

James Rorke's grave. Rorke requested he should be buried under 3ft of concrete to prevent his remains being disturbed – he then, according to local folklore, committed suicide. Historically, British graves have regularly attracted looting in the belief that white people were buried with their possessions.

The Oskarsberg terraces. Occupied by the Zulu marksmen during the battle. Following the battle, soldiers of the 24th carved their regimental number into the rocks. These engravings are still visible.

James Rorke's grave. (*Adrian Greaves*)

Chapter 10

Fort Pearson and the Skirmish at Fort Tenedos, 25 January 1879

The British plan for Colonel Pearson's Coastal Column was to march from Durban to the Tugela River, where a fortified supply depot could be garrisoned by the sailors of the Naval Brigade. From here, the column would advance as part of a pincer movement on Ulundi in conjunction with the other two columns. Once at Eshowe the column's supply wagons were to be unloaded and returned to the Tugela base to pick up more stores while defences were swiftly built to convert Eshowe into a fortified advanced supply depot. Pearson's first task was to move his men, transport and supplies across the swollen Tugela River. The overall plan was remarkably similar to that of the Centre Column, which was likewise using the mission station at Rorke's Drift as their forward base before advancing deeper into Zululand.

Meanwhile, the intermediate base for the assembling Coastal Column, Fort Pearson, named in honour of Colonel Pearson VC, was a strong fortification built on a high rocky prominence on the Natal bank overlooking the Tugela River and within sight of the Indian Ocean just 3 miles distant. Its commanding position must have appeared formidable to the Zulus as they looked across the 200 yards of fast-flowing river that separated the two countries. On 11 December 1878, Zulu envoys were ferried to the Natal riverside and presented with the findings of the Boundary Commission and then read the terms of the British ultimatum. After a lunch of roast beef, they were ferried back across the river to report to King Cetshwayo.

HMS *Tenedos* landed its detachment at Durban on the 1 January 1879, and they arrived at Fort Pearson on the 6th, increasing the column by 138 sailors under Commander (Acting Captain) Campbell and the marines under the command of Lieutenant Dowding.

On 11 January, after frustrating delays in assembling all his supplies across the river, Pearson's men of the Coastal Column were ready to cross the Tugela River, a task that took two days to complete, to much applause from the local

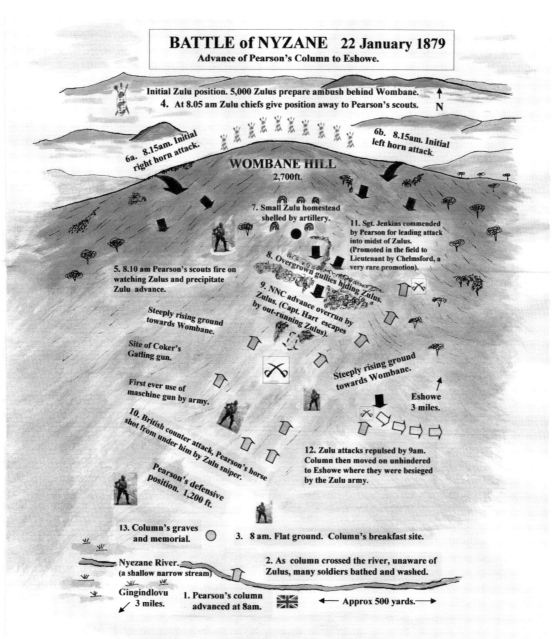

BATTLE of NYZANE   22 January 1879
Advance of Pearson's Column to Eshowe.

Initial Zulu position. 5,000 Zulus prepare ambush behind Wombane.
4. At 8.05 am Zulu chiefs give position away to Pearson's scouts.

N

6a. 8.15am. Initial right horn attack.

6b. 8.15am. Initial left horn attack.

WOMBANE HILL
2,700ft.

7. Small Zulu homestead shelled by artillery.

11. Sgt. Jenkins commended by Pearson for leading attack into midst of Zulus. (Promoted in the field to Lieutenant by Chelmsford, a very rare promotion).

5. 8.10 am Pearson's scouts fire on watching Zulus and precipitate Zulu advance.

8. Overgrown gullies hiding Zulus.

9. NNC advance overrun by Zulus. (Capt. Hart escapes by out-running Zulus).

Steeply rising ground towards Wombane.

Site of Coker's Gatling gun.

First ever use of maschine gun by army.

Steeply rising ground towards Wombane.

Eshowe 3 miles.

10. British counter attack, Pearson's horse shot from under him by Zulu sniper.

12. Zulu attacks repulsed by 9am. Column then moved on unhindered to Eshowe where they were besieged by the Zulu army.

Pearson's defensive position. 1,200 ft.

13. Column's graves and memorial.

3. 8 am. Flat ground. Column's breakfast site.

Nyezane River.
(a shallow narrow stream)

2. As column crossed the river, unaware of Zulus, many soldiers bathed and washed.

Gingindlovu
3 miles.

1. Pearson's column advanced at 8am.

◄— Approx 500 yards. —►

Tugela River - Ian Knight at site of Fort Pearson.

colonials who gathered on the high ground on the Natal bank, giving the scene, according to Commodore Norbury, 'the appearance of a gigantic picnic'. During that time, the Naval Brigade was engaged hauling the laden pont and ferrying men and materials across in the several boats they manned. On the morning of the 13th, all but seventy men of HMS *Active* and some from HMS *Tenedos* were ferried across the Tugela and onto Zulu soil. Those sailors left behind garrisoned Fort Pearson. Due to the time required to ferry Pearson's force across the Tugela River, a secondary holding fort, Fort Tenados, had been erected across the river as a temporary stores depot in mid-January by Captain Warren Wynne RE to protect the stores and troops being assembled for the invading column.

The fort, named after HMS *Tenados*, was octagonal with two gun positions, all with a good field of fire and protected by a wire entanglement around its perimeter. On 18 January, Pearson's column set off towards Ulundi – that very same morning, less than 100 miles away, identical orders were being followed by Colonel Pulleine at Isandlwana

Virtually unknown and mostly ignored is the incident that occurred at Fort Tenedos just a week after the column had departed towards Ulundi. On the night of 25 January, and with sentries posted, the men remaining at the fort had settled for the night when shots were fired by an unseen group of Zulus. The shots hitting the camp were sufficiently accurate to cause the defenders some concern, and they returned fire, shooting into the dark as a deterrence, and no doubt giving the defenders some courage. The exchange of fire lasted about an hour, but in the morning there was no sign of any dead or wounded Zulus. The Zulus may well have been part of a marauding *impi,* as a similar event occurred at Eshowe on the night of the 28th, again without any British casualties.

The column was a strong force that consisted of over 400 men of Pearson's 3rd (East Kent) Regiment (The Buffs), 160 of the 99th Duke of Edinburgh's (Lanarkshire) Regiment, 90 men from the Royal Engineers, 60 men of the Natal Native Pioneers, 115 of the Imperial Mounted Infantry and 117 Colonial troopers. The Royal Artillery consisted of twenty-two men with two 7-pounder guns. The bulk of the column consisted of another 1,655 officers and men from two battalions of the 2nd Regiment, NNC, who were not expected to fight as infantry but to scout and pursue a beaten foe. The Royal Engineers supplied 85 Sappers, and the 312 strong squadron of horsemen were made up from the Imperial Mounted Infantry, as well as the more colourfully-named local units from the Natal Hussars and the Mounted Rifles, from towns including Durban, Stanger, Victoria and Alexander. The total number of fighting men, according to the records of the day, was 4,397. In addition, 620 civilians were employed to drive the 384 ox wagons.

Pearson's force, now divided into two manageable columns with over 100 laden wagons between them, began its slow and laborious march to Eshowe, over a route quickly churned to a quagmire because of the heavy rains. With the two columns stretched out for several miles along the track, they were highly vulnerable to Zulu attack. Unbeknown to Pearson, a Zulu force of about 3,500 warriors had already been detached from Cetshwayo's main *impi* at Ulundi and was marching to intercept Pearson's struggling column. As they headed south, the approaching Zulus were joined by increasing numbers of warriors until they totalled more than 6,000, with others still to join.

On 21 January, Pearson was informed that a large force of Zulus was assembled at the royal homestead at nearby Gingindlovu.

Location
On the south bank of the Tugela River, the 1879 border of Natal with Zululand.

How to find it
From Durban. Take the R102 or the N2 northwards from Durban; turn off the motorway at the Zinkwazi Beach exit. Follow the signs to Tugela and the R102. On reaching the R102, turn right. After 5 miles (8km), take the right-hand turning signposted to the Ultimatum Tree and Fort Pearson. Report to the site office, then follow the dirt road for 3 miles (5km); Fort Euphorbia and Fort Pearson are on the obvious small hill to the left next to the river. Take the obvious left fork and drive to the top of the hill where there is adequate parking and a pleasant picnic spot next to the cemetery overlooking the Tugela River. Fort Pearson is 100 yards further along the track; it is located by the orientation hut in the centre of the fort. From the site of Fort Pearson, the Ultimatum Tree can easily be reached on foot by walking across the pedestrian bridge spanning the motorway – distance about 300 yards. Alternatively, one can drive to the car park at the site, which has been declared a National Monument and lies in the shade of the new but noisy motorway.

The Ultimatum Tree.

Distinguishing features

The Tugela River and the N2 motorway, which is immediately next to the site. Although the N2 motorway straddles the site, one must leave the motorway either side of the Tugela River and then follow the signs; there is no immediate access from the motorway to the location.

Points of interest

1. The Ultimatum Tree. This tree still survives in the form of the original stump, and strongly growing shoots. The site has been declared a National Monument. The Ultimatum Tree site is also the site of the river crossing used to ferry the Zulu chiefs to the reading of the Ultimatum, and to ferry troops across, using floating ponts.
2. Fort Pearson and orientation hut. The lines of defence and trenches are still clearly visible.
3. Fort Euphorbia, initially manned by the troops of HMS *Tenedos*. The original British cemetery can be found on the hill crest with Captain Wynne's grave. (He was the constructor of Fort Eshowe and Fort Tenedos.)
4. Second British cemetery where those who died of fever between the 1st and 2nd invasions are buried.
5. Fort Tenedos, on the Zulu bank of the river. It was named after HMS *Tenedos* and was also built by Captain Wynne RE for easier distribution of stores to the front line. The fort can be reached from the R102. Its outline can best be seen from Fort Pearson or Euphorbia Hill.

Chapter 11

The Battle of Nyezane, 22 January 1879

The Coastal Column's invasion of Zululand, led by Colonel Pearson, and its battle at Nyezane would forever be overshadowed by the fate of the Centre Column and subsequently neglected by historians. If the catastrophe at Isandlwana and the heroics of Rorke's Drift had not occurred, then the battle of Nyezane might well have been ranked by Britain's military establishments with the best known examples of British Army battles. In essence, it had all the ingredients to become a famous battle; instead, its battlefield and cemetery lie forgotten and are hardly ever visited or acknowledged by historians.

The British plan was to cross the river border into Zululand and advance inland to the mission station at Eshowe in order to establish a fortified supply depot. From here, the column would advance on Ulundi in conjunction with the other two columns.

Pearson had been given the role of marching the column firstly from Durban to the Tugela River and then along a further 37 miles of rough twisting track from the Lower Drift on the Tugela River to occupy the small abandoned mission station at Eshowe, hopefully before the Zulus destroyed the buildings. Here, the column's supply wagons were to be unloaded and returned to pick up more stores while defences were swiftly built to convert Eshowe into a fortified advanced supply depot. Pearson's first task was to move his men, transport and supplies across the swollen Tugela.

All in all, it was a formidable force and a logistical nightmare. Also accompanying the column were men from HMS *Active,* which landed its detachment at Durban on 19 November 1878, arriving at Fort Pearson on the 24th; HMS *Tenedos* landed its detachment at Durban on 1 January 1879, and they arrived on the 6th, increasing the column at Fort Pearson by 138 sailors under Commander (Acting Captain) Campbell and the marines under the command of Lieutenant Dowding. The naval contingent had marched from Durban with the rest of the column to enable the two ships to be reloaded with stores for Pearson's column. Indeed, it was sailors from HMS *Active* who

FORTS PEARSON and TENEDOS 1878-9

Approaches to Fort Pearson covered with broken glass and mined electrically. Spiked pits were built at strategic points.

ZULULAND

To Eshowe

N

St Andrew's Mission. (English—abandoned).

Barren ground.

1. 18 Jan. Local colonists gathered to watch the invasion.

3. On the night of 25 Jan. a Zulu raiding party fired on Fort Tenedos. No casualties were suffered.

Euphorbia cemetery.

Mounted force.

Fort hospital.

Naval Brigade and hospital.

Fort Tenedos

TUGELA RIVER Low sand islands.

Fast flowing deep water.

Steep cliffs

Natal Pioneers.

Stores.

Grassy scrub.

200 yards wide.

A steel hawser was laid across the river to enable easy pontoon access to Zulu river bank.

Fort Pearson

Seaman Martin from HMS *Tenados* was the first river casualty when he fell in and was lost.

HQ

Pont mooring

Tugela River

Buffs

Ultimatum Tree.

Pont bridge built across river in March 1879 for 2nd invasion.

2. On 11 Dec. 1878 Zulu envoys given the British ultimatum. After a lunch of roast beef they were ferried back across the river to report to King Cetshwayo.

2nd NNC.

99th Regt.

Smith's Hotel For traders and hunters pre-conflict.

Lower Tugela Drift.

RA

Fort Pearson had a clear view across the Tugela River into Zululand and to the Indian Ocean three miles distant.

Naval Bde.

Buffs.

Troops were aware of the presence of aggressive crocodiles and Hippos along the banks of the Tugela.

Fort Williamson

RE Coy.

Native Pioneers.

NATAL

NNC.

To Durban 55 miles.

1 mile.

Supplies landed from the sea.

INDIAN OCEAN

rowed the Zulu delegation across the Tugela, where they were presented with Frere's impossible demands when they gathered under the Ultimatum Tree on 11 December.

The crews were thoroughly schooled in both firearms and cutlass drill. In addition, *Active* supplied two 12-pounder Armstrong field guns, two rocket tubes and a Gatling gun. The latter had been carried on board during the Ashanti War, but this was to be the first time a machine gun would see use by the British in a land campaign.

Having assembled his forces, Pearson's first task was to move them across the Tugela, treacherously swollen by heavy rain, and establish a base on the opposite bank. The sailors rigged up a pontoon, repeatedly rowing across the fast-flowing river to carry cables to the Zulu bank. Meanwhile, under the supervision of a Royal Engineer officer, the ship's carpenters constructed the pont, designed by Colonel Durnford; this laborious task was accomplished in five days. The *Active* crew had brought with them one of the ship's bower anchors, which was used to secure the steel hawser on the far bank. It was during an effort to pull the heavy hawser through the fast moving current that Lieutenant Craigie slipped off the raft and was carried under the structure by the strong current; he was lucky to be dragged out, half-drowned but grateful for his lucky escape. Two of the *Active*'s sailors were also swept overboard from the raft. One was quickly rescued, but the other, Able Seaman Dan Martin, drowned, and his body was never recovered. He had the unenviable distinction of being the first casualty of the Zulu War. Two sailors jumped into the river to try and save Martin, but he could not be found; both were awarded a Royal Humane Society medal.

An improvised fortification was hurriedly prepared on the Zulu river bank to protect the crossing, which was manned by a small detachment of the naval contingent and named 'Fort Tenedos' after their ship.

Pearson's force, now divided into two columns with over 100 laden wagons between them, began its slow and laborious march to Eshowe, over a route quickly churned to a quagmire because of the heavy rains. With the two columns stretched out for several miles along the track, they were highly vulnerable to Zulu attack. Unbeknown to Pearson, a Zulu force of about 3,500 warriors had already been detached from Cetshwayo's main *impi* at Ulundi and was marching to intercept Pearson's struggling column. As they headed south, the approaching Zulus were joined by increasing numbers of warriors until they totalled more than 6,000, with others still to join.

On 21 January, Pearson was informed that about 4,000 to 5,000 warriors were assembled at the royal homestead at Gingindlovu; an attacking force was sent and, as the homestead was deserted, a good half an hour was spent by the troops setting the homestead on fire. This forced the now infuriated chief, Godide kaNdlela, to bring forward his original plan to attack the column. Unseen by the column scouts the Zulus withdrew behind the nearby hill, Wombane, a location of some significance for the Zulus, having been the setting of an earlier Zulu success against a Boer commando. Wombane was perfect for a Zulu ambush; the hill crest hid the massing Zulus and overlooks the Nyezane River. Through the mist at first light the Zulu scouts were able to look down on the advancing British column as it began crossing the river far below them.

Major Barrow's mounted scouts, unaware of the watching Zulus, waded through the knee-high water and followed a track until they came upon a fairly large open area approximately half a mile from the river. Beyond this point, the track climbed up a long spur leading to the crest of a high ridge. Extending from this ridge and running parallel either side of the track were two further spurs. The ravines between the three spurs were filled with tall, man-concealing grass. A third of the way up the central spur was a grassy knoll situated to the right of the track. Also to the right and dominating the ridge was the dome-shaped hill, Wombane. On the left of the track and near the summit, was a small native homestead of some twenty huts.

Some of the troops, who were not on guard duty, took the opportunity to bathe in the smaller streams that flowed down from the heights. At around 8am one of the vedettes reported to Barrow that a small party of Zulus had been seen gathering in the hills ahead. They were warriors from the Zulu left horn. The hill crest was still blocking the view of the gathering Zulu centre and right horn from the British. Barrow passed this information on to Colonel Pearson, who, disliking the idea of Zulus on his flank, immediately ordered the NNC to advance in order to drive them off. Led by Captain Fitzroy Hart, the NNC advanced up the track on the centre spur. A small party of Zulu scouts were then seen moving on the skyline before melting into the bush and reappearing on the lower slopes of Wombane to the right of the British.

Led by Hart, the NNC advanced up the hillside. The NNC officers, mainly locally recruited Germans, had no knowledge of their native troops' language, and the inevitable confusion soon ensued. The natives were clearly aware of the Zulus hiding in the long grass ahead of them and tried to warn their officers.

In turn, the officers could not understand their men's reluctance to advance and tried to urge them on. One even brandished his sword and yelled '*Baleka*' thinking it was Zulu for 'charge'. In fact, it means 'run'. The NNC needed no further encouragement; they turned to obey the order and ran back down the slope urgently seeking the protection of the ravine. At the same time, hundreds of Zulus emerged from behind the crest of the hill and fired a ragged volley before charging down on the rapidly retreating NNC. Some white officers and NCOs were rooted to the spot, either over-confident or with fear, and tried to hold their ground but were quickly overrun and killed. Hart did not stay to be slaughtered, and, being fleet of foot, managed to run back to safety.

The charge by the Zulu left horn was the premature attack of a carefully planned ambush, although the centre and right horn were not yet in position to pose an effective threat. The Mounted Volunteers quickly formed a firing line to the right of the track and fired into the left flank of the Zulu horn as they tried to work their way towards the wagons. Hart's men started to emerge from the undergrowth of the ravine, only to be met by 'friendly fire' until they were identified.

Pearson could see he was in a highly vulnerable position. His wagons were strung out for several miles behind the scene of the action, and the river was dividing his command. He was in no position to form an effective defence, and his only course of action was to rush as many reinforcements forward as possible. Fortunately, he already had with him his artillery, the guns and men of the Naval Brigade and two companies of The Buffs. As they were getting into position, the men of the Royal Engineers, who had been working at the stream crossing, joined the Mounted Volunteers on the firing line and helped keep the Zulus at bay.

The Zulus responded by advancing towards Pearson's column, leaving the British officers in no doubt that they were about to come under a serious attack. The rest of the Zulu *impi* now appeared on the ridge above. Pearson placed himself on the knoll with the artillery and his beloved Buffs; he then ordered both the Queen's and Regimental colours to be unfurled. The Zulus on the right had gone to ground and were putting down a heavy but inaccurate fire into the widespread British position; they were also crawling through the thick grass and getting closer to the defenders. Casualties on the British side were mounting, and some officers directed a concentrated fire on those Zulu sharpshooters who were causing the most damage. One casualty was Colonel Pearson's horse, which was badly wounded and had to be put down.

The 7-pounder guns and rocket tubes were dragged up the track to the grassy knoll, which gave them an excellent field of fire, and, soon to be assisted by a Gatling gun, quickly forced the Zulus to retreat back up the hill. The Gatling gun was still at the wagon, having previously sustained damage to its limber pole. It was rapidly repaired, and a 19-year-old midshipman, Lewis Coker, had it rushed up the track to the knoll. This young man had the distinction of supervising the first British use of the machine gun in a land battle, and he is believed to be the first midshipman ever to submit a report as a commanding officer. Sadly, he died of dysentery on 16 March.

The Zulus had prepared a careful ambush with their force of over 6,000 warriors that should have inflicted a severe defeat on the unprepared British, but their plan failed. For the British, a potential disaster became a stunning victory. There were no decorations or medals for this action, but one NCO, Sergeant Jenkins, received an immediate field promotion to Lieutenant for his bravery in leading a charge into the attacking Zulus.

How to find it

Route 1. From Durban. Route 68. Take either the R102 or the N2 motorway north from Durban. If travelling by motorway, take the first exit to Gingindlovu, which brings one onto the R102. Follow the signs to Gingindlovu. Remain on the R102, avoiding the town centre. Within a few hundred yards, take the left fork to Eshowe, the R68. The battlefield is only 1 mile (1.6km) from Gingindlovu and is situated on the left side of the road. A battlefield sign, stone memorial and the name of the farm, Kia-Ora, mark the entrance. Take this turning off the main road and follow the signs to the cemetery, which is 100 yards along the track.

Route 2. From Eshowe. Route 68. Follow the R68 southwards towards Gingindlovu until the route crosses the Nyezane stream. From this point, the battlefield is only 0.75 miles (1km) further on and is situated on the right. A battlefield sign and the name of the farm, Kia-Ora, mark the entrance. Take this turning off the main road and follow the signs to the cemetery, which is 100 yards along the track.

Modern memorial at Nyezane battlefield, now overgrown.

Distinguishing features

The only obvious feature of the battlefield is the prominent leaning pine tree next to the battlefield. This tree can easily be seen from both directions, and in early 2020 it was still a good marker point. Sadly, so much has changed since the battle. The battlefield is located in sugar cane fields; however, the cemetery is usually well maintained. A reasonable view of the battlefield can be gained from the cemetery itself.

Points of interest

1. The cemetery. Colonel Northey's remains were taken to England for re-burial.
2. Fort Eshowe is 12 miles (20km) to the north along the R68.
3. The battlefield of Nyezane is 10 miles (16km) to the north along the R68 and is clearly visible to the north.
4. The battlefield memorial.

Chapter 12

The Seventy-Two Day Siege of Eshowe

The Battle of Nyezane took place 100 miles due east of Isandlwana, but the victory was all but forgotten in the wake of that disaster. Pearson paused only to bury his own dead before ordering the march towards Eshowe to resume.

Rising at 3.00 am the next morning of 23 January, the column moved off and advanced the last 5 miles to Eshowe, which they reached at 10.00 am. Here they were pleasantly surprised to find the deserted mission station in good condition and complete with a garden filled with fruiting orange trees. The mission covered an area of 120 yards by 80 yards, sloping west to east; it had five abandoned but usable buildings, and there was a good supply of water from two nearby streams. Although the site seemed to be an excellent choice, the senior Royal Engineer, Captain Warren Wynne, had reservations. Despite being on high ground, the mission station was overlooked by higher ground, across a ravine filled with undergrowth and nests of poisonous snakes, right up to the mission's perimeter, which had to be made defensible.

Two days later, forty-eight of the empty wagons were escorted back to Fort Pearson to collect more stores. They passed another convoy en route to Eshowe and heard the first rumours that all was not well with the Centre Column and that Colonel Durnford and his NNC had been annihilated. It was not until the 28th that Pearson received a message from Chelmsford, brought by runner, that he was to prepare for the whole Zulu army to descend on him, or retreat back to Fort Tenedos. In the absence of firm information, Pearson took the unusual step of calling all officers to a council of war to decide whether to retreat or stay. Having endured both a gruelling battle and a difficult journey to occupy and fortify Eshowe, Pearson was reluctant to withdraw. Wynne also strongly advocated defending the position, fearing that a strung-out retreating column would present the Zulus with an easy target; Pearson decided to remain at Eshowe.

ESHOWE The 72 day siege.   23 Jan. to 4 April 1879.

1. Infestations of deadly puff-adders, mambas and other poisonous snakes had to be removed from the camp

5. The position was protected by an 8 ft high earthwork and surrounded by a deep moat like trench.

6.   1 March. To relieve the boredom, troops raided Chief eSiqwakene's nearby homestead. Due to the presence of the Zulus around the fort, disturbing false alarms were a nightly feature and although large bodies of Zulus were regularly seen, none actually approached the fort.

7. During the siege, five court-martials were held for disobedience of orders and three floggings were ordered. One soldier drowned himself in a puddle.

Wire perimeter

Water store.

Spiked pits

Cattle pen.

Officers' bathing pool.

Fort Eshowe

Store.

Church & Hospital.

Soldiers' bathing pool.

2. Wire entanglements were stretched from stakes hidden in the long grass so that any attack would be slowed once the Zulus entered within range of the garrison's weapons.

On a clear day the soldiers could see the sea 23 miles distant.

Access to the fort was via a wooden drawbridge.

← 100 yds. →

9. Garrison cemetery. 28 of the garrison are buried here, mainly fever cases.

10.   Eshowe never came under direct Zulu threat. To maintain morale, the camp social life included cricket, tennis and concerts - which the Zulus enjoyed from a distance - and lectures.

8. 9 April. In mid-March Capt. Wynne contracted fever and was moved to Fort Pearson where he died on 9 April. It was his birthday, and the date of his promotion to major.

3. At night the Zulus removed posts marking a new roadway under construction from the fort. Wynne and his sappers resolved this particular irritation by mining the posts with explosives.

4. Firing platforms for the cannon and Gatling gun were constructed at the angles of the ramparts while drawbridges were built at the two gates. All in all, the fort at Eshowe became an impressive looking fortress and was the most sophisticated of the 99 British earthwork forts built during the entire war.

He recognized that the mounted men and the NNC were unnecessary in such a defensive position, and feeding them would be difficult if supplies were interrupted. He ordered Major Barrow to take his force, with some NNC, back to Fort Tenedos; this reduced the strength of the Eshowe garrison to 1,460 combatants and about 335 civilians. The remaining cattle were laagered alongside the entrenchment until it dawned upon the defenders that it was a noisome health hazard. Nearly 1,800 men were now effectively under siege with no immediate prospect of receiving supplies or reinforcements. Pearson ordered the commissariat to put the garrison on three-quarter rations. King Cetshwayo was so infuriated that Pearson's column had settled at Eshowe that he ordered the Zulu regiments in the area to surround the British position and prevent their withdrawal. Within days, the Zulus had completely surrounded the British and settled down to watch the proceedings and in the afternoons listen to the bands playing. From 5 February, the regimental band of the 3rd (East Kent) Regiment (The Buffs) played every afternoon.

By the second week of February, Captain Wynne had loop-holed all the buildings and ordered a deep ditch to be dug around the perimeter, with earth piled inside to form a defensive rampart. During the coming weeks, he added traverses to stop the possibility of Zulu rifle fire raking the interior lines, while 'trous-de-loup', known by the soldiers as 'wolf-pits', were dug in the ground with upwards pointed stakes placed in the bottom; these were built across the three approaches to the fort.

On the 28 February, the remaining NNC element were permitted to leave Eshowe, which they did in haste and wildly retreated back to Natal, causing much comment in both civilian and military circles. The *Natal Colonist* published that the rout was due to the poor leadership of Major Graves. He sued the newspaper in October and won £100 damages for libel, then a year's pay for a major.

The stifling hot weather eventually broke, and heavy tropical rain added to the soldiers' miseries. Everyone was constantly soaked through and with no available shelter, sickness quickly spread among the men. The garrison had sufficient food and plenty of ammunition, but it lacked adequate medical supplies, and on 1 February the first man died of fever. The heavy rains turned the area within the entrenchment into a thick quagmire of effluent polluted mud that added to the growing discomfort and weakening health of the garrison's 1,700 men. To supplement the men's reduced rations, Pearson encouraged foraging patrols to plunder local deserted Zulu homesteads in the hope of finding additional food, although the garrison's meagre rations held out until Eshowe was relieved. After working in the oppressive heat of the day, the men had to sleep as best they could under the wagons, as there was no room to erect their tents within the encampment. Without tents, everyone was constantly soaked, and, as a result, sickness broke out. False alarms often interrupted their sleep and demoralized them. Large bodies of Zulus were regularly seen, but none approached Eshowe.

The heavy rains caused the area within the entrenchment to become a sea of deep mud that added to the garrison's discomfort. News of Isandlwana was brought by runners on 2 February and plunged everyone into a state of shocked depression. At last, they learned the truth of the fate of the Centre Column. It is indicative of the problem of communications that it took twelve days to acquaint Pearson with news of the disaster. One wonders, if he had known days earlier, whether he would have ordered a withdrawal back to the Lower Drift. Instead, nearly 1,800 men were effectively under siege with no immediate prospect of receiving supplies or reinforcements.

Meanwhile, work continued on the defences, and by the second week of February, Captain Wynne had turned the hastily built entrenchment into a formidable-looking fortress. The whole area was now surrounded by a deep, wide ditch and was further protected by a 6ft high defensive wall. Firing platforms for the cannon and Gatling guns were constructed at the angles of the ramparts, and drawbridges were built at the two gates.

Conscious of the danger of sickness in such an overcrowded area, Pearson gave great attention to preventing their fresh water from becoming polluted and to siting and rotating the latrine area downhill away from the camp. Despite these precautions, the overpowering stench within the camp and from the nearby cattle laager became increasingly offensive, attracting clouds of flies that infested the garrison's food supplies. The general health of the men rapidly deteriorated, with the majority of soldiers suffering from serious stomach disorders. By the end of February, seven men had died, including one suicide by drowning in a muddy puddle. Unsanitary conditions, exposure and a lack of appropriate medicines caused a steady decline in the health and morale of the defenders.

Apart from an occasional skirmish with the outlying vedettes, the Zulus kept their distance but constantly made their presence known. An estimated 5,000 Zulus were in the immediate vicinity, but, having learned from their experience at Rorke's Drift, were not inclined to attack such a well-defended position.

Instead, they maintained a loose mobile ring of some 500 warriors to watch and harry the defenders in the hope that starvation would force them into the open where they would be vulnerable to attack.

Frequent heavy storms worsened the situation, while incessant strong winds battered the fort. During one storm at the end of the month, the Naval Brigade's position was all but washed away by a flash flood, which also seriously damaged the parapet. The livestock had exhausted all the grass near the fort and now had to be sent further afield to graze. This necessitated strong escorts drawn from The Buffs, the 99th and the Bluejackets, who disliked this tedious detail. The monotony was often broken by the watching Zulus taunting and shouting insults at them.

As supplies diminished, the meagre rations consisting of hard biscuits, mealies and stringy meat, were further reduced. This depressing state of affairs was relieved somewhat by Colonel Pearson ordering the auction of rations left behind by the Mounted Volunteers. It is a measure of how desperate the besieged troops had become for a change from the monotonous food that defenders were prepared to pay highly inflated prices for items like a jar of pickles or a tin of cocoa. Pearson estimated that £7 worth of goods fetched in excess of £100. Looking further to raise flagging spirits, Colonel Pearson led a 500-strong night raid on 1 March to a Zulu homestead a few miles distant. Just before dawn, as they manoeuvred into position, a lone Zulu raised the alarm. Nevertheless, the faltering attack commenced. Although sixty-two huts were burned and the artillery inflicted some casualties, Pearson's men had to make a fighting retreat for several hours before they reached the safety of the fort.

The next day brought a more lasting boost to morale. One of the mounted vedettes noticed a distant bright flashing light coming from the direction of

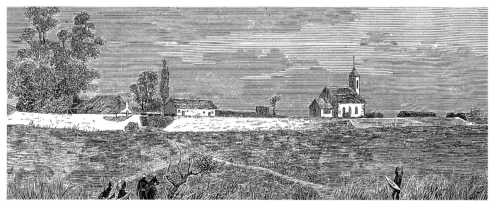

The fort at Eshowe. (*Illustrated London News*)

the Lower Drift. It took a while to realize that it was an improvised heliograph sending out a signal to establish communications with Eshowe. At last, Pearson and the garrison were informed that the Zulus had not overrun Natal and that help could soon be on the way. Although the heliograph was available, no such signalling equipment had been used to date in this war. By using a mirror borrowed from a local settler, the men on the Fort Pearson promontory were finally able to establish contact. In response, the Eshowe garrison tried a variety of unsuccessful signalling methods, ranging from a large moveable screen that sent Morse code messages, to making a hot air balloon that was expected to drift all the way to the border. After six weeks of siege, Wynne succeeded in sending some signals by means of a carefully positioned piece of lead piping taken from the church roof and an officer's shaving mirror. In the end they were able to fashion their own heliograph, which was successful. It took four frustrating days to get a cloud-interrupted message through to Pearson that his wife had given birth to a son. It also advised him that a 1,000-strong column would be setting off on 13 March to relieve him.

Meanwhile, Chelmsford and his staff were busy with preparations for the second invasion of Zululand, but before these could be finalized, the relief of Eshowe would be essential. Chelmsford was powerless to relieve Eshowe until he received additional troops from Britain; the garrison had to fend for itself. During early March, Chelmsford built up a strong enough force to attempt Pearson's relief, and Eshowe was relieved on 7 April. To the disgust of the defenders, Chelmsford ordered Eshowe be abandoned to the Zulus.

Between 23 January and the 3 April, twenty-six men died, mostly of fever, including five of the Naval Brigade. Especially mourned was Midshipman Coker, the Gatling gun commander who had fever and yet insisted on sleeping by the Gatling, covered only by a greatcoat. Others who died of disease in March included Lieutenant and Adjutant Davison 99th Regiment, Lieutenant Evelyn and Captain Williams of The Buffs; Evelyn had carried the Colours at Nyzane. A total of twenty-eight members of the garrison succumbed to disease and were buried just 100 yards from the site of Fort Eshowe. Captain Wynne RE died of fever on 9 April, his thirty-sixth birthday and the date of his promotion to Major. His grave is in the fort's cemetery overlooking the Tugela River.

Location
The nearest town is Eshowe, which has all the usual amenities of an average-sized town.

How to find it

Route 1. From Durban. Take the R102 or N2 motorway north from Durban. If travelling by motorway, take the first exit to Eshowe and Gingindlovu, which brings one onto the R102. Follow the signs to Eshowe and Gingindlovu. On approaching the town of Gingindlovu, remain on the R102 that bypasses the town centre. Within a few hundred yards, take the left fork to Eshowe, the R66. After passing the Gingindlovu battlefield on the left side of the road, remain on the R66. After crossing the Nyezane stream, Wombane Hill will begin to dominate the road from the right-hand side. There is a battlefield marker on the left-hand side of the road that indicates the site of the memorial to those killed in the battle. The memorial is about 250 yards down this track on the right-hand side; follow the pathway for a few yards to the memorial. It is best to park off the road to explore this battlefield.

Route 2. From Eshowe. Route 68. Follow the R68 southwards towards Gingindlovu for 2 miles (3.2km). The road will then begin to drop down towards the plain, and Wombane Hill will appear and dominate the left-hand view. Look out for a battlefield marker on the right-hand side of the road and pull off the road on to the dirt road. The battlefield marker on the right-hand side of the road indicates the site of the memorial to those killed in the battle. The memorial is about 250 yards down this track on the right-hand side; follow the pathway for a few yards to the memorial. It is best to park off the road to explore this battlefield.

Distinguishing features

The only obvious feature of the battlefield is Wombane Hill in conjunction with the battlefield sign on the main road.

Recommendations

A competent guide is essential if exploring this battlefield. It covers a wide area, and there are no remaining features to be seen of the battle itself. The battlefield from the Nyezane River to the British 'form up' point is usually covered in sugar cane. From the R68 road across to Wombane Hill, the route to the base of the hill is through very rough scrub before the long sharp climb to the top of Wombane Hill can be undertaken. Nyezane is a battlefield for the very fit enthusiast only, unless the visitor is content to view the scene from the graves or the roadside.

Points of interest
1. The memorial and graves of the British dead.
2. Wombane Hill.
3. Fort Eshowe is 2 miles (3.2km) to the north along the R68.
4. The battlefield of Gingindlovu is 10 miles (16km) to the south along the R68.

Chapter 13

Ntombe River (Meyer's Drift), 12 March 1879

'No particular precautions appear to have been taken'.[4]

This engagement marked the second Zulu victory over the British and involved Colonel Wood's Northern Column. Following his unexpected defeat by the Zulus, the first three months of 1879 were a living nightmare for Lord Chelmsford and his command.

Chelmsford knew that he needed Wood's Northern Column, unaffected by the Centre Column's withdrawal to Natal, to harass the northern Zulus, particularly the abaQulusi tribe. This aggressive and large Zulu force had somehow to be discouraged from marching to Ulundi to support King Cetshwayo's main army, or, alternatively, prevented them moving south, nearer to Natal, and threatening the colony. Although the abaQulusi were not strictly within the Zulu military system, they were considered by both King Cetshwayo and the British to be part of the Zulu nation. They dominated a large part of the territory through which Chelmsford was planning to advance his second invasion force. Their stronghold was a 4-mile-long, almost inaccessible, flat-topped mountain known as Hlobane.

On 1 February, while leading a cattle raiding expedition, Buller discovered, attacked and destroyed an important Zulu homestead situated 30 miles east of the British camp at Khambula. Buller's mounted force captured some 300 head of cattle and destroyed the homestead's 250 huts; a number of Zulus were killed in the raid without any losses to Buller. In angry response, Prince Mbilini waMswati, a pro-Zulu prince of Swazi origin, Manyanyoba and two chiefs of the Ntombe Valley district led marauding parties of Zulus into the neighbourhood of Luneburg, now abandoned by the white farmers due to marauding Zulu *impies*, and commenced an appalling massacre of the local tribesmen who had previously worked for white farmers. Their wives and children were especially

---

4. Survivor's report, *British Battles on Land and Sea*, Cassell, 1898.

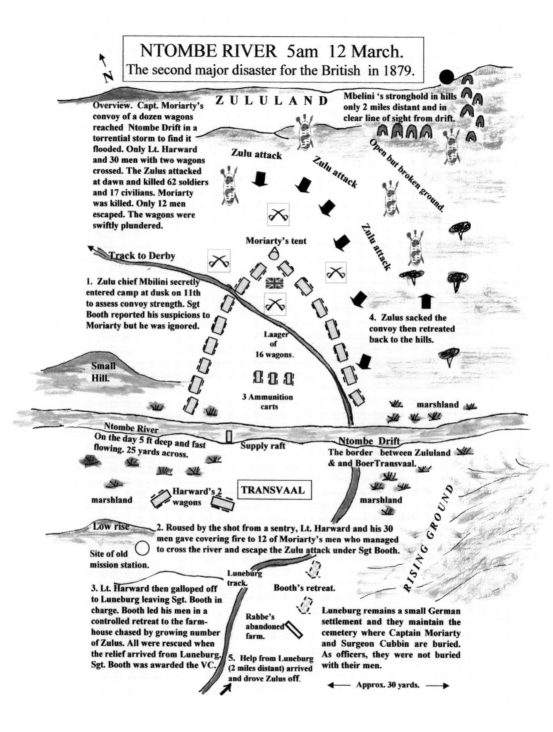

NTOMBE RIVER 5am 12 March.
The second major disaster for the British in 1879.

ZULULAND

Overview. Capt. Moriarty's convoy of a dozen wagons reached Ntombe Drift in a torrential storm to find it flooded. Only Lt. Harward and 30 men with two wagons crossed. The Zulus attacked at dawn and killed 62 soldiers and 17 civilians. Moriarty was killed. Only 12 men escaped. The wagons were swiftly plundered.

Mbelini 's stronghold in hills only 2 miles distant and in clear line of sight from drift.

Open but broken ground.

Zulu attack

Moriarty's tent

Track to Derby

1. Zulu chief Mbilini secretly entered camp at dusk on 11th to assess convoy strength. Sgt Booth reported his suspicions to Moriarty but he was ignored.

Laager of 16 wagons.

Small Hill.

4. Zulus sacked the convoy then retreated back to the hills.

3 Ammunition carts

marshland

Ntombe River
On the day 5 ft deep and fast flowing. 25 yards across.

Supply raft

Ntombe Drift
The border between Zululand & and Boer Transvaal.

marshland

TRANSVAAL

Harward's 2 wagons

marshland

Low rise

Site of old mission station.

2. Roused by the shot from a sentry, Lt. Harward and his 30 men gave covering fire to 12 of Moriarty's men who managed to cross the river and escape the Zulu attack under Sgt Booth.

Luneburg track.

Booth's retreat.

3. Lt. Harward then galloped off to Luneburg leaving Sgt. Booth in charge. Booth led his men in a controlled retreat to the farmhouse chased by growing number of Zulus. All were rescued when the relief arrived from Luneburg. Sgt. Booth was awarded the VC.

Rahbe's abandoned farm.

5. Help from Luneburg (2 miles distant) arrived and drove Zulus off.

Luneburg remains a small German settlement and they maintain the cemetery where Captain Moriarty and Surgeon Cubbin are buried. As officers, they were not buried with their men.

RISING GROUND

← Approx. 30 yards. →

brutalized, killed either with spears or by being burnt alive in their huts.

On 13 February, Buller led a fresh mounted force to undertake retaliatory measures, destroying five of the less well defended homesteads; 34 Zulus were slain and a herd of 400 cattle was captured.

Hitherto, the area along the Transvaal border to the north of Hlobane had not caused Chelmsford any real concern, so by the end of February, the border-watching 80th Regiment had moved from Derby to their new post at Luneburg, where Major Tucker was in command, though stores and ammunition still needed to be brought from Derby. The route from Derby crossed the Ntombe River, only 4 miles

Memorial to 80th Regiment at Ntombe Drift.

from Tucker's base at Luneburg and within sight of the mountainous stronghold of Mbilini. Due to the proximity of the Zulus, who were well known for their raiding abilities, convoys from Derby required strong escorts, and so Tucker's companies were rotated to march out to meet the wagons and to bring them safely to Luneburg.

On 1 March, 'D' Company under Captain Anderson marched from Luneburg and linked up with a floundering 20-strong wagon train bringing the garrison urgently needed supplies from Derby along with 90,000 rounds of Martini-Henry ammunition. Progress was painfully slow as the torrential rain had persisted for days on end, making the track virtually impassable. The wagons had to be manhandled most of the way and continually sank to their axles in thick mud. After four days of toil, the men were plastered in mud, cold and badly exhausted. Anderson then received an ambiguous message from Tucker, which he interpreted as a recall to Luneburg. He gratefully took his men, leaving the floundering convoy in command of Lieutenant Lindop all but unprotected. A small force of Mbelini's warriors had been shadowing the convoy and when they realized that there was no escort, they seized their chance and helped themselves from the helpless and bogged down wagon train. They ignored the few protesting wagoners and made off with a small amount of stores and some oxen, with the intention that they would return in strength to seize the remainder of the supplies.

When Anderson arrived back at Luneburg without the wagons, Tucker was horrified and immediately ordered out a fresh company of 106 men under Captain David Moriarty to escort them to safety. By 11 March, the river was in flood and totally impassable, but Lindop's weary men had somehow managed to bring two wagons across the river to the relative safety of the south bank. Moriarty's force helped recover the remaining seventeen wagons, and after two days of backbreaking work, the wagons were finally brought to the crossing point on the Zulu north bank of the river. Meanwhile, the river had burst its banks, preventing them from crossing until the water level subsided. Moriarty ordered the wagons to be laagered in a protective 'V' formation, with the two legs reaching the water's edge. The ongoing heavy rain had caused the river to flood beyond its normal 30-yard width and to a depth of over 9ft.

During the afternoon, Major Tucker, accompanied by Lieutenant Henry Harward, Sergeant Anthony Booth and thirty-two soldiers, arrived at the river crossing to assess the situation. Tucker found a bedraggled company of utterly exhausted men and the bulk of their convoy of wagons still firmly trapped by the high water on the far bank. He realized that they had laboured in continuous rain for four days without cooked food, but he could do little to ease their predicament. He made suggestions for the wagons to be laagered correctly, although he noticed that there were growing gaps between the wagons and the river where the high water level had slowly begun to recede. Although exhausted and highly vulnerable to attack, Tucker may have presumed that, as they were only 4 miles from their destination, the danger from attack was minimal. Instead of assuming command, he ordered Moriarty to remain in command but replaced Lindop and his exhausted men with Harward's force. Tucker then returned to Luneburg.

Using an improvised raft, Harward and his men crossed the river to help Moriarty secure the camp. Some cattle had wandered off and been seized by watching Zulus, so Harward took a small search party and recovered the cattle, killing a number of Zulus responsible for the loss. By the end of the day, the two wagons on the south bank were guarded by Harward, Sergeant Booth and thirty-four men. There were still seventeen wagons on the north (Zulu) bank arranged in a defensive 'V' formation under the guard of Captain Moriarty and the remaining seventy-one men.

All settled down for the evening and began to have dinner. One of the European drivers drew Sergeant Booth's attention to an unknown black man eating corn and talking with some of the wagon auxiliaries. The driver expressed the opinion that this stranger was none other than Prince Mbilini; it was widely known that his stronghold was less than 3 miles way. Booth reported his suspicion to Moriarty, who assured him that the locals were friendly. Moriarty added, 'You're as bad as your pals said of you; you would shoot your own brother.' Booth, an experienced 33-year-old NCO, was later to write that he was not reassured and believed that, Mbilini or otherwise, the stranger was there to spy out the defences.

The interior of the north bank wagon laager covered little more than half an acre and was filled with the soldiers' tents and oxen. Moriarty gave instructions for just two sentries and even felt safe enough to pitch his tent outside the noisome confines of the laager. Meanwhile, Harward, having skirmished with a small group of Zulus and collected the stray cattle, felt tired enough to stretch out in Captain Moriarty's tent. Amiable as Moriarty was, he had no intention of sharing his accommodation and sent Harward back across the river to his own command on the south bank. Moriarty's exhausted men, tired and wet, stripped off their clothes, washed in the river and fell into a deep sleep under shelter for the first time in days. On the south side of the river, Harward's camp was also fast asleep when, at about 4.00 am Harward was awakened by the sound of, so he thought, a distant shot. Noticing that the sentries could not be seen and that no one on the north bank had stirred, he took the precaution of ordering Booth to alert the north bank. Booth eventually managed to spread the warning, but it had little effect and both camps slept on.

The previous night's unexpected visitor, whether it was Mbilini or one of his scouts, had disturbed Booth. Sufficiently alarmed, he quickly got dressed and, taking his rifle and ammunition pouch, climbed into one of the wagons for a smoke. Booth had every reason to feel uneasy for, unbeknown to the sleeping soldiers, Mbilini had mustered 1,000 warriors and silently advanced upon the camp under cover of the early morning mist. Having observed the exhausted soldiers the previous day, the Zulus were expecting little resistance, and most carried only their stabbing spears and knobkerries.

At about 4.45 am, another shot was heard, causing Booth to jump from the wagon just as the massed Zulus emerged from the mist. Now less than 50 yards from the British position, the leading Zulus fired a ragged volley into Moriarty's tents, and then their packed ranks charged at the tents, and within seconds they were into the sleeping camp. Moriarty dashed from his tent, firing his revolver at the warriors closing in upon him. He felled three before an assegai thrust finished him, and, with that, he and most of his men died. Bemused and naked soldiers had struggled from their tents only to be clubbed or stabbed to death in the nightmare of frightened cattle and terrified men. Some soldiers managed to plunge naked into the river and several managed to reach the south bank, now manned by Harward, Booth and a few men who attempted to cover their colleagues escape with steady rifle fire.

Booth quickly rallied his small command and they commenced a sustained fire into the mass of Zulus on the far bank. Booth noticed that he was next to Lieutenant Harward's horse, which was tied to the wagon. Harward then appeared from his tent and shouted out, 'Fire away, lads, I'll be ready in a minute!' He then mounted his unsaddled pony and rode off towards Luneburg, followed by an undisciplined surge of most of his men leaving Booth with only eight of his company. While he and his small group calmly kept up a steady rate of fire, some of the men who had crossed the river managed to arm themselves with abandoned rifles and joined Booth's group. Within moments, Booth realized his position was hopeless, and, assisted by Lance Corporal Burgess, they formed the remaining men into a tight square and prepared to retreat, back-to-back, towards Luneburg. Booth was later complimented for choosing to form a square rather than the more commonly used extended line.

Thankfully for Booth, the Zulus were more intent on plundering the wagons than pursuing his men, although about twenty Zulus made a number of concerted efforts to overwhelm the small square. Booth controlled his men's rate of fire while keeping the square moving, and they painfully made their way towards a deserted farmhouse that Booth had seen about a mile distant. Four men who panicked and fled the group were promptly run down and killed by the Zulus, but Booth managed to bring his remaining handful of men to the protection of the farm building.

Meanwhile, Lieutenant Harward had galloped the short distance to Luneburg, where he arrived at 6.30 am. He roused Major Tucker and blurted out the news:

The camp is in the hands of the enemy; they are all slaughtered, and I have galloped in for my life.[5]

Tucker ordered 150 men to turn out and quick-march towards the Drift, then immediately left on horseback, accompanied by several of his mounted officers, and within minutes they came upon Booth's party at the farmhouse, causing the remaining Zulus to flee. Booth gallantly volunteered to accompany Tucker's command back to the river, but his offer was declined – he had done enough having protected his small band all the way from the river.

As Tucker's men reached the rise overlooking the river, they saw hundreds of Zulus moving away from the camp in the direction of their nearby stronghold. Most were laden with plunder. On riding into the wrecked camp, they discovered that all their colleagues, one officer, one doctor, sixty-four soldiers and fifteen black levies were all dead, naked and mostly disembowelled. Some twenty soldiers were missing and presumed drowned in the fast-flowing river. The Zulus had killed all the dogs, scattered mealies and flour and shredded the tents; all 300 camp cattle had been driven off. When the marching relief duly arrived, Tucker set them to work collecting the mutilated bodies, ferrying them across the river and burying them on the slope overlooking the crossing. As they were officers, the bodies of Captain Moriarty and the company's 28-year-old civilian doctor, William Cobbin, were taken back to the hamlet at Luneburg for individual burial. The number of dead Zulus was estimated at about twenty.

In the aftermath of the disaster at Isandlwana, there followed a considerable amount of 'covering up' of facts, and this new engagement was no different; there was an enforced regimental 'agreement' not to speak about the engagement at Ntombe. To help conceal the embarrassment of his actions, Lieutenant Harward's official report stated that:

The enemy were now assegaing our men in the water, and also ascending the banks of the river close to us; for fear therefore, of my men being stabbed under the wagons, and to enable them to retire before their ammunition should be exhausted, I ordered them to retire steadily, and only just in time to avoid a rush of Zulus to our late position. The Zulus came on in dense masses and fell upon our men, who, being already broken, gave way, and a

---

5. Sir Evelyn Wood's Papers.

hand-to-hand fight ensued. I endeavoured to rally my men, but they were too much scattered, and finding re-formation impossible, I mounted my horse and galloped into Luneburg at utmost speed, and reported all that had taken place.

Likewise, Major Tucker praised Harward's efforts in giving covering fire to enable some men to escape across the river. These two reports were the basis of Lord Chelmsford's report to the War Office, which was not received in London until the 21 April. Up to this point, the circumstances surrounding Harward's desertion of his men were contained within the regiment. The final death toll was put at eighty-six British and fifteen black levies. As Colour Sergeant Henry Fredericks had been killed in the incident, Booth was confirmed in the rank of colour sergeant to replace him.

At Ulundi the 80th formed part of the massive square that finally broke the Zulu fighting spirit, and during the engagement the regiment sustained two dead and five wounded. Amazingly, and despite seeing much action throughout a long military career, the only injury Booth ever sustained was when a stray a bullet struck his mess tin. Booth received some metal splinters in his face, his only war wound in a long military career.

At the end of the year, the regiment was stationed at Pretoria, and it was from here, on 20 December, that three survivors of the Ntombe engagement wrote to General Sir Garnet Wolseley to 'set the record straight to be of service to Colour Sergeant Booth'. There was a great deal of mounting anger throughout the regiment that certain facts been suppressed by various officers. Wolseley began to ask embarrassing questions and Tucker finally had to explain that the report at the time should have revealed the 'far different conduct of Lieutenant Harward'. On the 26 December, the whole regiment was paraded prior to leaving for England. Wolseley took the salute, and, in a most unusual ceremony, presented Colour Sergeant Booth with a revolver, holster, belt and a knife, which were all donated by grateful European settlers. On the same day, Wolseley forwarded his personal recommendation that Booth should be awarded the Victoria Cross. This was an exceptional gesture, as Wolseley had been highly critical of the number of VC awards during the campaign.

On 14 February, as a result of Wolseley's investigations, Lieutenant Harward was arrested and taken to Pietermaritzburg, where he was charged with two offences:

1. having misbehaved before the enemy, in shamefully abandoning a party of the regiment under his command when attacked by the enemy, and in riding off at speed from his men;
2. conduct to the prejudice of good order and military discipline in having at the place and time mentioned in the first charge, neglected to take proper precautions for the safety of a party of a Regiment under his command when attacked.

The court martial was held at Fort Napier in Pietermaritzburg, and much to the surprise of many and the fury of Wolseley, the court acquitted Harward of all charges, and he was allowed to return to his regiment. Wolseley could not alter the verdict, but he refused to confirm the court's findings, adding his own view:

Had I released this officer without making any remarks upon the verdict in question, it would have been a tacit acknowledgement that I had concurred in what appears to me a monstrous theory, viz. that a Regimental Officer who is the only Officer present with a party of men actually and seriously engaged with the enemy, can, under any pretext whatever, be justified in deserting them, and by so doing, abandoning them to their fate. The more helpless a position in which an officer finds his men, the more it is his bounden duty to stay and share their fortune, whether good or ill. It is because the British officer has always done so that he possesses the influence he does in the ranks of our army. The soldier has learned to feel, that come what may, he can in the direst moment of danger look with implicit faith to his officer, knowing he will never desert him under any possible circumstances.

When the findings and Wolseley's comments reached The Duke of Cambridge, Commander-in-Chief of the Army, he instructed them to be read out as a general order to every regiment throughout the British Empire. With his army career in tatters, Harward had little option but to resign his commission, which he did on arriving at King's Town on 11 May 1880.

On 26 June 1880, Colour Sergeant Booth was summoned from Ireland to Windsor Castle, where the Queen presented him with the Victoria Cross. The citation reads:

For his gallant conduct on the 12th March 1879, during the Zulu attack on the Ntombe River, in having when considerably outnumbered by the enemy, rallied a few men on the south bank of the river, and covered the retreat of fifty soldiers and others for a distance of three miles. The officer Commanding 80th Regiment reports that, had it not been for the coolness displayed by this non-commissioned officer, not one man would have escaped.

Booth's conduct and that of another 80th man, Private Samuel Wassall, who received the only Isandlwana Victoria Cross at Fugitives' Drift, gave the regiment justifiable pride in what had been a less than glorious campaign. In one final gesture of atonement to cover Harward's deed, his name was expunged from the 80th Regiment's records, a most unusual act for an infantry regiment of the line.

The Battle of Ntombe was yet another British disaster brought about by poor planning and a total unwillingness of senior officers to heed good intelligence while in enemy territory, especially as British experience fighting Zulus since January had been calamitous.

Location
The nearest town is Paulpietersburg, which has all the facilities of a small town.

How to find it
From Vryheid. Take the R33 north from Vryheid to Commondale, and then take the left turn due west towards Luneburg. From Commondale, stay on the road for 16 miles (25km), and then take the left turn to Luneburg itself. After 1 mile there is a battlefield marker post to the left, indicating the Ntombe battlefield. Follow the dirt road for half a mile and approach the modern, tall spired church situated on a small rise. Go past the church, and the battlefield cemetery will be to the front. The actual battlefield is situated on both sides of the river, just 200 yards beyond the cemetery. In dry conditions the river can be crossed on foot to where the main British force was attacked. Lieutenant Harward defended the nearside of the river before he left his men to get help.

British cemetery at Ntombe Drift.

Distinguishing features

Ntombe battlefield is off the beaten track and therefore necessitates considerable determination to reach it. The services of a guide should be sought, as this battlefield lies well off the road and cannot be seen from the R33. Follow the signs from the road and then look for the very stark-looking church.

Recommendations

Park on the high ground beyond the church and walk to the cemetery. The drift is further down the slope at the river, which is partially hidden by trees.

Points of interest

1. The British cemetery dedicated to the 80th Staffordshire Regiment. The cemetery was severely damaged in 2000 by vandals.
2. The river bank where Moriarty and most of his men camped, and were killed by the Zulus.
3. The river bank commanded by Lieutenant Harward.
4. Route taken by survivors under command of Sergeant Booth.
5. Direction of the nearby small German settlement at Luneburg and the cemetery where Captain Moriarty and Surgeon Cubbin are buried. As

officers, they were not buried with their men. The church in Luneburg is also well worth visiting. The residents of Luneburg always make visitors welcome.

In 2020, the half-mile track from the road to the battlefield was only negotiable on foot or by four-wheel drive vehicles. The British cemetery had, yet again, been extensively vandalized and today lies sadly neglected. Significantly, a small posy of roses had been laid on the memorial during the previous year. The faded card reads, 'God bless my Great-grandfather and his colleagues who died here'. The great-grandfather would have been proud that his descendent had made the laudable effort to get there to pay their respects.

Chapter 14

Hlobane, 28 March 1879

Following news of the British defeat at Isandlwana, Colonel Wood moved his force to the hilltop fort at Khambula, which, over the next few weeks, was strongly fortified. By March, Chelmsford was well advanced with his plans for the relief of the besieged Eshowe garrison, but it was essential that the belligerent abaQulusi Zulus to the north should first be neutralized. Chelmsford could not risk having such a powerful force within striking distance of his invasion route for the second invasion and instructed Wood to destroy the Zulu stronghold at Hlobane, just 20 miles away.

On 27 March, Wood dispatched two groups to attack Hlobane led by Colonels Buller and Russell respectively. The force under Buller consisted of 400 mounted men, all local volunteer horsemen except for a few imperial officers, and 280 black auxiliaries. Included in the horsemen were the Border Horse, commanded by an experienced ex-cavalry officer, Lieutenant Colonel Frederic Weatherley, who had fought in both the Crimean War and the Indian Mutiny. Russell's force was made up of 200 mounted troops and 440 black auxiliaries, plus 200 dissident Zulu warriors who had defected to the British under Prince Hamu, a half-brother of King Cetshwayo. Russell would attack Hlobane from the easily accessed lower adjoining plateau of Ntendeka, intending to meet up with Buller on the flat top of Hlobane. For the troops, there was the added incentive of a rich cash prize of over 4,000 Zulu cattle that grazed the flat mountain top.

The Zulus had originally intended to attack Wood at Khambula, but at dawn on the 28th, they realized Buller was progressively trapping himself on Hlobane and advanced to surround his force, the successful Isandlwana tactic, intending to continue on to Khambula next day. The Zulu force was 20,000 strong. Seeing the rapidly approaching Zulu army, the abaQulusi Zulus on the nearby Ityenka hill rushed to join the attack as Buller's force slowly progressed across the Hlobane Plateau, unaware they were being surrounded.

The attack on Hlobane was ill-conceived. Although Buller had skirmished with the Hlobane Zulus on 22 January, the plateau had not been subjected to

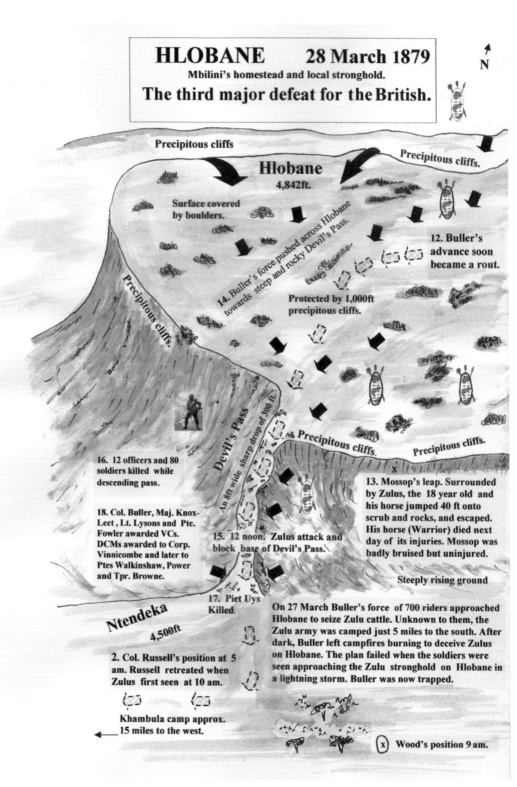

HLOBANE   28 March 1879

Mbilini's homestead and local stronghold.

The third major defeat for the British.

N

Precipitous cliffs

Precipitous cliffs.

Hlobane
4,842ft.

Surface covered
by boulders.

14. Buller's force pushed across Hlobane towards steep and rocky Devil's Pass.

12. Buller's
advance soon
became a rout.

Protected by 1,000ft
precipitous cliffs.

Precipitous cliffs.

Devil's Pass

An 8ft wide sharp drop of 300 ft.

Precipitous cliffs.

Precipitous cliffs.

16. 12 officers and 80
soldiers killed while
descending pass.

18. Col. Buller, Maj. Knox-
Leet , Lt. Lysons and Pte.
Fowler awarded VCs.
DCMs awarded to Corp.
Vinnicombe and later to
Ptes Walkinshaw, Power
and Tpr. Browne.

13. Mossop's leap. Surrounded
by Zulus, the 18 year old and
his horse jumped 40 ft onto
scrub and rocks, and escaped.
His horse (Warrior) died next
day of its injuries. Mossop was
badly bruised but uninjured.

15. 12 noon. Zulus attack and
block base of Devil's Pass.

Steeply rising ground

17. Piet Uys
Killed.

Ntendeka
4,500ft.

On 27 March Buller's force of 700 riders approached
Hlobane to seize Zulu cattle. Unknown to them, the
Zulu army was camped just 5 miles to the south. After
dark, Buller left campfires burning to deceive Zulus
on Hlobane. The plan failed when the soldiers were
seen approaching the Zulu stronghold on Hlobane in
a lightning storm. Buller was now trapped.

2. Col. Russell's position at 5
am. Russell retreated when
Zulus first seen at 10 am.

Khambula camp approx.
15 miles to the west.

x Wood's position 9 am.

ITYENKA

ITYENKA NEK

Precipitous cliffs

Cliffs 400ft high.

Precipitous cliffs

4,450ft.

11. Lts. Barton and Poole climbed down cliff to escape but 5 miles from Hlobane were caught by Zulus and killed. The location of their graves remains unknown.

8. Weatherley's force trapped on nek by Zulus. 5 Officers and 40 men killed, some thrown off cliffs. Barton's burial party over-whelmed, Barton escaped.

10. abaQulusi Zulus joined attack from Ityenka as Buller's force advanced across Hlobane.

Steep rising ground.

Narrow Pass

Deep caves.

Precipitous cliffs

7. Zulus withdrew into caves only to re-emerge behind Buller's force. Buller unaware of rapidly approaching Zulu army from south.

Precipitous cliffs

Steep cattle track, some horses lost.

9. 11am. Capt. Campbell & Mr. Lloyd in Wood's party killed by Zulu snipers. Wood then retreated and went 'missing' for 8 hours abandoning Buller on Hlobane. His whereabouts remain unknown.

6. On night of 27/28th Col. Weatherley's scouts under Capt. Dennison had discovered Zulu camp and warned Col. Wood who dismissed account on grounds it was 'nonsence'. Dennison then refused to co-operate with Wood and withdrew his men under accurate sniper fire from Zulus in caves.

4. Buller's move hindered by severe thunderstorm. Lightning illuminated his advancing men and warned Zulu who bombarded them with boulders and point-blank gunfire.

3. Col. Buller's night advance to Hlobane left camp fires burning in failed attempt to decoy Zulus.

5. Advancing Zulus' camp just five miles from Hlobane. Zulus intended to attack Khambula first but at 9 am. Zulus realised Buller would be trapped on Hlobane and advanced to surround his force, as at Isandlwana, intending then to continue on to Khambula next day. Zulu force 20,000.

← Approx. 1 mile. →

any reconnaissance, and the routes up and down were unknown to the British, who presumed they offered 'easy' routes off the plateau's unseen northern side. The flat but rock-strewn top of Hlobane is 4 miles long and 1 mile wide. It is generally 500ft above the surrounding plain, and, apart from three precipitous pathways known only to the Zulus, the flat top mountain is virtually inaccessible.

The original intention of Wood's two-pronged attack was to take the Hlobane Zulus by surprise. At dusk, Buller lit campfires on the plain to give the Zulus the impression that he was bypassing Hlobane and that the real target of his column was the Zulu army. Fatally, for most of his men, Buller wrongly presumed the Zulu army to be advancing from Ulundi. In the early hours, Buller and his men began to move towards Hlobane, leaving their campfires burning to deceive the Zulus.

Buller's move against Hlobane, undertaken in a violent thunderstorm under cover of darkness, was made difficult by stone breastworks that had been constructed by the Zulus at the top of the rough cattle tracks to hinder just such an attack. Buller's advancing force was fired upon from these breastworks, and some casualties were incurred; boulders were also rolled down on the advancing British force struggling up the steep path. At dawn, and successfully on top, Buller was still unaware of the close proximity of the approaching Zulu army, now less than 5 miles away. Buller left A Company at the top of the path as a rearguard and detached Lieutenant Barton to bury the dead who had been killed on the ascent. The defending Zulus had disappeared into a number of caves, enabling the British to loot their cattle as they slowly headed to the far end of the plateau to meet up with Russell. Unbeknown to Buller, Russell had arrived at the bottom of the precipitous pass linking the two plateaus, forbiddingly known as the 'Devil's Pass', and found his route to the top blocked by its steepness.

Meanwhile, in the confusion and darkness, Weatherley and his Border Horse missed Buller's departing column and spent most of the night trying to find it. In fact, while themselves lost, Weatherley's scouts under Captain Dennison had inadvertently discovered the encamped Zulu army, and at 9.00 am the following day, Dennison found Colonel Wood and his small escort gathered at the base of Hlobane, anticipating watching Buller's force seize Zulu cattle. The group was completely unaware of the swiftly approaching Zulu army. Dennison breathlessly warned Wood of the Zulu's imminent arrival, to which Wood retorted, 'nonsense' and turned away. Wood then ordered Weatherly to take

View from R69 of Hlobane and Devil's Pass.

his men and join Buller on Hlobane. Fuming at the rebuff, Dennison refused to co-operate with Wood and withdrew his men, just as the group came under Zulu sniper fire from a cave entrance above them. A Zulu marksman then shot Mr Llewellyn Lloyd, Wood's political officer. His body was recovered by Captain Ronald Campbell, Wood's staff officer, and carried a short distance to a stone cattle kraal, where Wood's escort and the Border Horse were sheltering. Wood ordered the Border Horse forward, but they alleged the position was unassailable and refused. Campbell went forward with a few of Wood's escort but was shot dead as he reached the snipers' cave.

Meanwhile, the Zulus on Hlobane had seen Russell's column heading for the far western end of the mountain and correctly anticipated that their stronghold was to be attacked from both ends. Knowing that their main Zulu army was fast approaching they left their caves and attacked Buller's men. They quickly recovered their cattle and routed A Company, forcing Buller's whole force towards the lip of the treacherous Devil's Pass; Buller's men were now aware of the main Zulu army moving to encircle them. On seeing the massed ranks of Zulus rapidly approaching the base of Hlobane, both British columns panicked. On the lower plateau of Ntendeka, Russell received an ambiguous message from Wood, who, misunderstanding his map of Hlobane, ordered

Route to Devil's Pass on Hlobane Mountain.

Russell to move to an irrelevant location 5 miles from the scene. With the Zulus fast approaching his force, Russell and his men departed as fast as they could ride, controversially abandoning Buller and his men now, converging at the top of Holbane's Devil's Pass.

Beneath the cliffs, and still unaware of the fast-approaching main Zulu army, Wood and his personal staff officers met up with Weatherley and the Border Horse, who were clearly lost; Wood ordered them to climb Hlobane to support Buller. Hardly had the two parties met when they were fired upon by Zulus hiding in a cave, causing the Border Horse, who were leading, to take cover.

With the Zulu army now in sight and fast approaching his position, a visibly confused Wood and his remaining escort rapidly rode away from Hlobane, narrowly escaping the advancing Zulu army and then going 'missing' for eight hours.

Meanwhile, Barton and his men, who had earlier been detailed as a burial party, and Weatherley's force that was still trying to join Buller's force, were

Top of Devil's Pass on Hlobane Mountain.

caught and slain by the approaching Zulus. Barton managed to get his horse off the precipitous north side of the plateau and, while riding away, came across Lieutenant Poole of the Border Horse, now on foot. Barton took Poole on his horse and the pair set off, trailed by a party of Zulus. The pair were eventually caught and killed on the bank of the Manzana River, 8 miles from the scene of their escape.

With the Zulu army now visible, Captain Dennison, Weatherley's deputy, who had found the Zulu army a few hours earlier and had reported their presence to Wood, independently took his men off towards the Ntendeka *nek* to support Buller. Chased and trapped by the Zulus against the edge of a cliff, and with no alternative escape, Dennison attempted to lead his men down the steep cliff face, but most fell or were speared by the Zulus. Dennison and three of his men reached the base, and, having found three riderless horses, set off for Khambula. On arrival, Dennison reported to Buller with his account; Buller requested Dennison to 'say nothing and lie low', which Dennison did out of respect for Buller. Wood never made reference to knowing of the Zulu advance on Hlobane.

Now trapped at the top of the Devil's Pass, Buller ordered the Zulu cattle to be abandoned, and, ignoring the steepness of the pass, ordered his men over the edge. Many men and horses fell to their deaths while descending. Yet, worse was about to happen; Zulus from the main force now reached the base of the pass and began firing into the slowly descending soldiers. As the survivors neared the bottom of the pass, the Zulus closed in on them, stabbing them with assegais. Having remounted, Buller and several of his officers did what they could to hold off the attacking Zulus; they even rode back to rescue men whose horses had been killed. In the end, only those who survived the Devil's Pass and still had horses could flee for their lives back to Khambula.

One trooper of the FLH, 18-year-old George Mossop, had climbed down the Devil's Pass without his horse, Warrior, and was ordered back by Buller to the top to re-mount. Having found his horse, he was pushed towards the edge of a 50ft cliff and, about to be rushed by Zulus, rather than be speared to death, he jumped off the cliff with his horse landing amidst trees and boulders. Both survived the fall and made it back to Khambula, although the horse died of its injuries the following day.

Wood eventually arrived at Khambula at dusk to learn of the disastrous day. His reaction to the news of Buller's defeat was not recorded, and Wood's whereabouts during the day remain a mystery.

Location
See Chapter 6, The First Battle of Hlobane, for directions. The only graves that can still be found, with difficulty, are those of Campbell and Lloyd. A guide will be needed to locate them, as they are neglected and hard to find. There is a memorial on the cliff edge where Weatherley's men were forced over the cliff by attacking Zulus. There is no cemetery, although this battle was a major defeat for the British, in which they, and the Zulus, suffered many casualties.

At the base of Devil's Pass are the remains of the Piet Uys memorial, sadly regularly vandalized.

Chapter 15

Battle of Khambula, 29 March 1879

This battle was one of the most important of the whole Anglo-Zulu War. Its outcome convinced Chelmsford that he could defeat the Zulus and persuade King Cetshwayo that he had lost the war.

After the ill-conceived British attack on Hlobane, and their defeat at the hands of the Zulus, Buller's few survivors were forced to flee for their lives back to the main British fortified hilltop position at Khambula, 20 miles to the north. Those who had lost their horses in the battle were quickly chased down and killed. The Zulu force that inflicted the defeat at Hlobane was, by coincidence, and unbeknown to the British, already en route to attack the British at Khambula.

After their victory at Hlobane, the Zulus were understandably confident of further victory and, after resting overnight in the area of the present-day town of Vryheid, they set off towards Khambula, just 10 miles to the north. When in sight of the distant British hilltop position the Zulus paused to take stock of the situation. The younger warriors convinced the senior chiefs that they should attack the British while they were still recovering from their savage mauling the previous day at Hlobane. In the British camp, Wood and his officers feared the Zulus would bypass their position to attack the British base at Utrecht. But the Zulus had already decided to attack the seemingly small force of British on the Khambula hilltop and, adopting the successful Isandlwana tactic, divided their army into three main columns that rapidly spread out in the typical Zulu attacking formation several miles wide.

Wood remained calm and, with the approaching Zulus now visible 5 miles away, prepared his force for the onslaught. Following a substantial meal at 12.00 pm, the tents were struck to give everyone a clear field of fire across the battlefield.

The Zulu plan was to initially attack the small British hill redoubt on two fronts, the classic 'horns of the bull' tactic, with the main body then attacking between the two flanks. Accordingly, the left horn approached the British hill

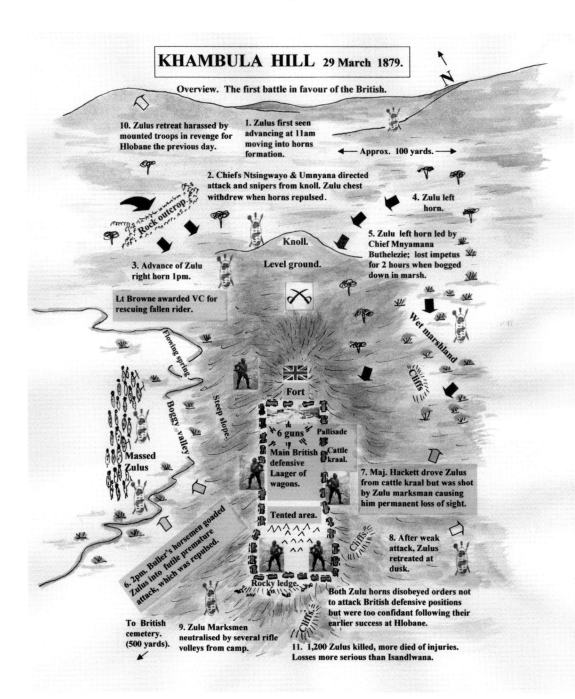

KHAMBULA HILL 29 March 1879.

Overview. The first battle in favour of the British.

N

10. Zulus retreat harassed by mounted troops in revenge for Hlobane the previous day.

1. Zulus first seen advancing at 11am moving into horns formation.

← Approx. 100 yards. →

2. Chiefs Ntsingwayo & Umnyana directed attack and snipers from knoll. Zulu chest withdrew when horns repulsed.

4. Zulu left horn.

Rock outcrop

Knoll.

Level ground.

5. Zulu left horn led by Chief Mnyamana Buthelezie; lost impetus for 2 hours when bogged down in marsh.

3. Advance of Zulu right horn 1pm.

Lt Browne awarded VC for rescuing fallen rider.

Wet marshland

Flowing spring.

Cliffs.

Boggy valley

Steep slope.

Fort

Massed Zulus

6 guns   Pallisade

Main British defensive Laager of wagons.

Cattle kraal.

7. Maj. Hackett drove Zulus from cattle kraal but was shot by Zulu marksman causing him permanent loss of sight.

Tented area.

Cliffs.

6. 2pm. Buller's horsemen goaded Zulus into futile premature attack, which was repulsed.

8. After weak attack, Zulus retreated at dusk.

Rocky ledge.

Cliffs.

To British cemetery. (500 yards).

9. Zulu Marksmen neutralised by several rifle volleys from camp.

Both Zulu horns disobeyed orders not to attack British defensive positions but were too confidant following their earlier success at Hlobane.

11. 1,200 Zulus killed, more died of injuries. Losses more serious than Isandlwana.

Khambula.

position along the course of a valley stream but became bogged down in soft marshland 2 miles distant. The right horn meanwhile arrived at its pre-attack position without being able to see the plight of the left horn. Buller recognized the opportunity and led his mounted men out of the British lines to within 200 yards of the waiting Zulu right horn. His men fired several volleys into the packed Zulu ranks, which was sufficient to provoke the Zulus to charge. Buller and his men then raced back to camp as the artillery opened fire over their heads and into the charging Zulus. Several of Buller's men were overtaken by the Zulus and killed, and it was at this point that Lieutenant Browne won his Victoria Cross for returning into the charging Zulus to rescue an unseated soldier. Due to controlled rifle and artillery fire, the Zulus were unable to reach the British position and took enormous casualties, so retreated.

The Zulu left horn then arrived and massed to attack, but, with the right horn now defeated and retreating, the British were able to concentrate their fire against the assembled warriors. The centre body of Zulus could not begin their attack due to the concentrated and accurate British firepower and contented themselves with sniping at the redoubt. An element of the left horn did reach the British cattle kraal but were beaten back by Major Hackett and a company of the 1/13th Regiment with fixed bayonets. Hackett was shot in the head by a Zulu marksman – he lost his sight but survived. By 5.00 pm the battle was over and the Zulus began their retreat. Buller and his riders then rode out from the camp and turned the Zulu retreat into a rout; they killed as many of the Zulus as they could find until darkness fell. Sergeant Jervis wrote home on 31 March.

> I confess that I do not think that a braver lot of men than our enemies in point of disregard for life, and for their bravery under fire, could be found anywhere. We were all employed burying the dead yesterday, and we had not finished by dark, pits being made three-quarters of a mile from camp, and the dead taken in carts. A more horrible sight than the enemy's dead, where they felt the effects of shellfire, I never saw. Bodies lying cut in halves, heads taken off, and other features in connection with the dead made a sight more ghastly than I ever thought of.

Participants
Colonel Wood's force totalled 2,086 officers and men and represented the following units:

Imperial: The Royal Artillery, Royal Engineers, 1/13th (Somerset) Light Infantry, the 90th Light Infantry and Imperial Mounted Infantry.

Colonial: Baker's Horse, Border Horse, Frontier Light Horse, Kaffrarian Rifles, Mounted Basutos, Raaf's Transvaal Rangers and Wood's irregulars.

Zulus: The Zulu force consisted of some 20,000 warriors and was commanded by two senior *indunas*, Ntshingwayo and Mnyamana Buthelezi. The right horn consisted of the iNgobamakhosi; the left horn, the uMcijo; the centre force, the uDloko, uDududu, imBube, uThulwana and the inDlondlo. Most of these units had fought at Isandlwana. Many units of the local abaQulusi had joined the Zulu force.

Casualties
Imperial: 3 officers and 26 men killed and 5 officers and 50 men wounded.

Zulu: At least 1,200 Zulus were killed around the battlefield. Many more died from their injuries post battle.

How to find it

From the town of Vryheid. Take the R33 northwards for 10 miles (16km) towards Paulpietersburg. The road runs through a blue gum tree forest, and the first indication of the battlefield will be the battlefield marker post on the left-hand side, indicating the route to the left. Follow the sign along the dirt road for about 1 mile (1.6km) to a junction, when another battlefield sign will indicate the dirt road to the left. After about another 2 miles (3.2km), the hill redoubt will become obvious to the front. About 500 yards from the position, the track passes through an old gateway, and in January 2002, there was a village football field with goalposts to the right of the track.

Distinguishing features

This battlefield lies well off the main road and cannot be seen from the R33. On arrival at the hill redoubt, climb the short distance to the crest; at this point, all the features of the battlefield can clearly be seen, as can the British cemetery, which lies 800 yards further along the pot-holed track to the west. Once at the site of the hill redoubt, all points of the battlefield can be reached on foot. It is sometimes possible to take a car to the cemetery, but this is not advisable in wet conditions.

Khambula memorial.

Recommendations

Khambula is an important battlefield in the historical sense, but it is an infrequently visited site, as it lies off the beaten track. It is a difficult place to visit in the rainy season and in wet conditions visitors would be advised to take a reputable guide; most guides use four-wheel drive vehicles that can deal with waterlogged and rough tracks. This battlefield is generally considered to be well worth the effort of getting there. Khambula is a truly splendid battlefield. It is easy to relate what happened onto the topography.

Chapter 16

Battle of Gingindlovu and the Relief of Eshowe, 2 April 1879

Pearson was now well established at Eshowe. On 28 January he received a remarkable message from Chelmsford, bravely brought by a despatch runner who had slipped through Zulu lines. Inexplicably, it did not mention the catastrophe at Isandlwana, but stated that Chelmsford had pulled back to Natal and that Pearson was to prepare for the whole Zulu army to descend on him.

Although surrounded by the cautious out-of-range Zulus, Pearson was powerless to intervene. To maintain morale, Pearson detailed burning forays against nearby Zulu homesteads. One such destroyed homestead belonged to Prince Dabulamanzi, but this action merely infuriated the Zulus into harassing Pearson's patrols with greater determination.

By early March Chelmsford had assembled a strong enough force to attempt Pearson's relief. On 29 March the relief column was ferried by ponts across the Tugela River into Zululand. The column began its advance further to the east than the obviously difficult route originally taken by Pearson, and it travelled light. No tents or baggage were allowed even though it was known that the column would suffer from the heavy rain and intolerable heat that marked late summer in Zululand. Chelmsford's scouts reported that the Zulus were gathering in considerable numbers to oppose his relief column near the abandoned Zulu village of Gingindlovu. The force consisted of the same Zulus who had so successfully besieged Eshowe, and now reinforced by regiments from Ulundi under the command of Chiefs Somopho kaZikhala and Phalane kaMdinwa.

Now more cautious, Chelmsford chose more open country, where he could laager his wagons and entrench each night. He further ordered that open ammunition boxes were to be readily available on the wagons. Once he reached Eshowe, Chelmsford's plan was to relieve the garrison and replace them with fresh troops and supplies.

The progress of the column was slowed by torrential rain that appeared each evening, swelling the rivers and streams; now, churning wagon wheels turned

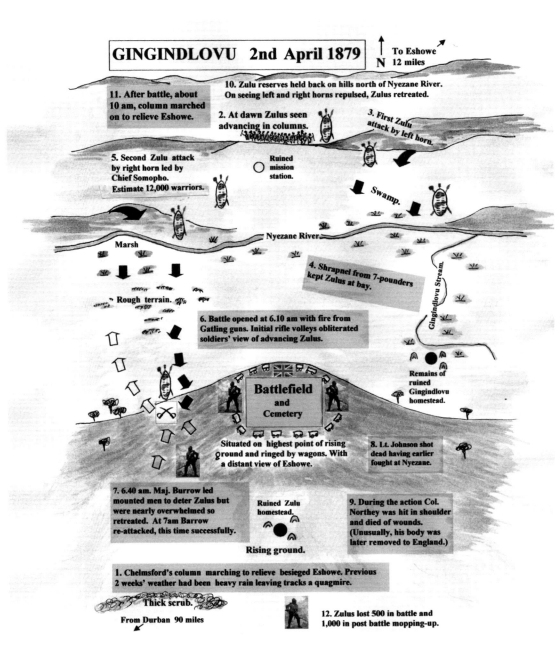

GINGINDLOVU   2nd April 1879   N   To Eshowe 12 miles

10. Zulu reserves held back on hills north of Nyezane River. On seeing left and right horns repulsed, Zulus retreated.

11. After battle, about 10 am, column marched on to relieve Eshowe.

2. At dawn Zulus seen advancing in columns.

3. First Zulu attack by left horn.

5. Second Zulu attack by right horn led by Chief Somopho. Estimate 12,000 warriors.

Ruined mission station.

Swamp.

Marsh

Nyezane River.

4. Shrapnel from 7-pounders kept Zulus at bay.

Gingindlovu Stream.

Rough terrain.

6. Battle opened at 6.10 am with fire from Gatling guns. Initial rifle volleys obliterated soldiers' view of advancing Zulus.

Remains of ruined Gingindlovu homestead.

Battlefield and Cemetery

Situated on highest point of rising ground and ringed by wagons. With a distant view of Eshowe.

8. Lt. Johnson shot dead having earlier fought at Nyezane.

7. 6.40 am. Maj. Burrow led mounted men to deter Zulus but were nearly overwhelmed so retreated. At 7am Barrow re-attacked, this time successfully.

Ruined Zulu homestead.

9. During the action Col. Northey was hit in shoulder and died of wounds. (Unusually, his body was later removed to England.)

Rising ground.

1. Chelmsford's column marching to relieve besieged Eshowe. Previous 2 weeks' weather had been heavy rain leaving tracks a quagmire.

Thick scrub.

From Durban 90 miles

12. Zulus lost 500 in battle and 1,000 in post battle mopping-up.

the thick mud along the track into a morass. Due to the adverse weather, early attempts at laagering were chaotic, and officers and men alike had to sleep on the ground totally unprotected from the incessant downpours. By the third evening, a simpler system had been devised so that each laager would be a square 130 yards each side, made up of thirty wagons butted together, all the livestock placed within, deploying the artillery and Gatling guns at each corner.

On the evening of 1 April, Chelmsford's rain-soaked column formed a square laager on the top of a low rise leading from the southern bank of the Nyezane stream. It was close to the ruins of Gingindlovu, the Zulu homestead that Pearson had attacked on the way to Eshowe, and in sight of Pearson's earlier Battle of Nyezane on 22 January. Knowing that a force of Zulus had detached from those surrounding Eshowe and was fast approaching, and having learned his lesson at Isandlwana, Chelmsford ordered the column's wagons to be parked in a tight square with a trench dug around the outside of the wagons. As dawn broke over the Nyezane valley, the scene was partially obscured by a hanging mist. At 5.00 am, Major Barrow's mounted scouts rode out and soon ran into the advancing Zulu scouts. Their firing as they retreated back to camp alerted the soldiers in the laager, who prepared for the gathering onslaught. Then, about 2 miles off, through the gaps in the mist, several large columns of Zulus could be seen advancing towards the camp from the direction of the stream and forming into their 'horns' battle formation.

Chelmsford's men were urgently rushed to man the barricades with orders to fire volleys at a range of no more than 300 yards. The battle was opened at 6.10 am by a siting burst from a Gatling gun, followed by a number of well-aimed volleys, which cut through the advancing Zulus. In the still of the early morning, the British were soon enveloped in dense smoke from their own volleys and were forced to cease firing until the light breeze cleared their view. Meanwhile, some 10 miles distant, those in the beleaguered fort at Eshowe keenly followed the opening moves of the battle through their telescopes and binoculars.

Undeterred, the Zulus sought to surround the British and steadily advanced through the tall grass towards the north side of the position defended mainly by young and inexperienced recruits of the 3/60th Rifles. It was a terrifying moment for these soldiers, who had been regaled with gruesome stories of the slaughter at Isandlwana; now they were confronted by the same seemingly irresistible charging horde of fearless warriors. Lieutenant Colonel Francis

Northey was hit in the shoulder and taken to the ambulance. Northey insisted on returning to the firing line, but the bullet had penetrated an artery, and he collapsed, haemorrhaging through his dressing. He died on 6 April.

The Zulu right horn then attacked the south wall occupied by the new recruits of the 91st Highlanders who beat off the attack. The remnants of this attack moved round to launch a final assault on the east side of the laager, which was defended by the older and more experienced men of the 57th, whose steady firing prevented any warrior getting close. Due to the main Zulu force advancing through very long grass, those defenders atop the wagons had a better field of fire and inflicted many casualties. As the Zulu attack appeared to falter, Chelmsford prematurely ordered Barrow's mounted troops out of the laager to drive off the warriors, only to hastily recall them when he saw they were in danger of being surrounded.

As the shrapnel from the 7-pounders continued to take its toll, the Zulus' assault on the square slackened. Unable to break through the British defences, they lost their momentum and began to retreat to the comparative safety of the long grass and some nearby clumps of palm bushes. The officers then directed their men's fire into the groups of hiding Zulus. This had the effect of killing a large number, forcing the survivors to flee back towards the stream and Wombane Hill from where the Zulu chiefs and reserves were observing the battle. The final shots were fired at 7.15 am, just as the Zulu reserves on Wombane, seeing their force beaten, also withdrew.

Finally, after an hour's fighting, Chelmsford re-ordered Major Barrow to drive the remaining Zulus further away from the laager. They were followed into the fray by the riders of the Natal Carbineers, who rode out with alacrity, cutting down exhausted and wounded warriors without mercy. The rest of the day was spent burying their dead and reducing the size of the laager. Chelmsford decided to leave a reduced laager and press on to Eshowe with a flying column.

Meanwhile, those in Eshowe with telescopes and binoculars keenly followed the battle. Pearson ordered congratulations to be flashed to Chelmsford and the garrison waited impatiently to be relieved. Chelmsford's men finally reached Eshowe, but Chelmsford had already changed his mind and decided that Eshowe was too exposed to hold. Accordingly, he proceeded to Eshowe with a smaller fast-moving column, leaving the remainder of the relief column at the Gingindlovu laager. Chelmsford and his reduced force arrived at Eshowe early that evening and were enthusiastically welcomed by the besieged garrison, but the defenders were aghast to learn that Chelmsford would abandon the fort instead of replacing it with a fresh garrison.

Chelmsford ordered the abandonment of Eshowe and marched its garrison after Pearson's column. The ever-watchful Zulus then entered the deserted mission and razed what was left to the ground. Catching up with Pearson, Chelmsford ordered him to head back by the most direct route to the Lower Drift, which he reached on 7 April.

It was during the march to Fort Pearson that a tragedy occurred. In the early hours of 6 April, an outlying piquet beyond Chelmsford's overnight halt at the eMvutsheni mission thought he saw Zulus in the pre-dawn gloom, and after his challenge went unanswered, fired a warning shot. This caused the remaining piquet to rush back into Chelmsford's laager. The retreat was so precipitate that some of the 60th Rifles abandoned not only their officers, but even their helmets. As the camp 'stood to', dark figures carrying shields and spears were seen running towards them. They were met with the bayonet as they tried to force their way into the camp; two were killed and eight more wounded. They were not Zulus but retainers of Chelmsford's intelligence officer, John Dunn, who had been posted in an advance screen beyond the camp. Chelmsford was furious, and convened a General Court Martial, which stripped a sergeant of the 60th of his rank and sentenced him to five years' penal servitude. The sentence was never carried out.

Chelmsford was fulsome in his praise for the tenacious Colonel Pearson, who was now suffering typhoid and was sent back to England to recover. He was made a Companion of the Bath. His men were well pleased with the outcome of the two battles that had dealt the Zulus a severe blow; there were awards for bravery and some personal reputations enhanced.

Although the opening British volleys against the Zulus had commenced at 400 yards, few bodies were found beyond 200 yards. The wisdom of ineffective opening fire beyond 200 yards began to be questioned by front line officers. In common with other battles of the war, the battlefield of Gingindlovu, once abandoned by the British, was left to the ravages of the elements and wild animals. Today the battlefield straddles the main coastal road to Ulundi, and the site is marked by a grey granite memorial on the roadside that lists the names of the dead – but the cemetery and site of Chelmsford's command post lies along a sandy track about a quarter mile from the road. Like most other military cemeteries from the war, it is overgrown and neglected. The sole reason

After the Battle of Gingindlovu. (*Illustrated London News*)

for its existence is due to the cemetery having been used as a burial ground by local white farmers who occasionally tend their family graves. Of the battlefield there is no sign. The whole area is now a sugar plantation, and for most of the year, the battlefield is hidden by impenetrable growing sugar cane.

Gingindlovu stuck in everyone's mind due to its onomatopoeic sounding name and became easily remembered by soldiers and civilians alike by the name 'gin gin I love you'.

Participants
Imperial. Commanded by Lieutenant General Lord Chelmsford. The 1st Brigade under Colonel Law included units from the Royal Artillery, Naval Brigade (HMS *Shah* and *Tenedos*) 91st Highlanders, 3rd Regiment The Buffs, 99th Duke of Edinburgh's Regiment. The 2nd Brigade under Lieutenant Colonel Pemberton included units from the Royal Artillery, Naval Brigade from HMS *Boadicea*, 57th West Middlesex Regiment and the 60th Rifles. Total: 3,390 white officers and men.

Colonial. 4th and 5th Battalions NNC. Total: 2,280 black troops.

Casualties
2 officers and 9 men were killed, with 4 officers and 46 men wounded.

Location
Route 1. From Durban. Route 68. Take either the R102 or the N2 motorway north from Durban. If travelling by motorway, take the first exit to Gingindlovu, which brings one onto the R102. Follow the signs to Gingindlovu. Remain on the R102, avoiding the town centre. Within a few hundred yards, take the left fork to Eshowe, the R68. The battlefield is only 1 mile (1.6km) from Gingindlovu and is situated on the left side of the road. A battlefield sign, stone memorial and the name of the farm, Kia-Ora, mark the entrance. Take this turning off the main road and follow the signs to the cemetery, which is 100 yards along the track.

Route 2. From Eshowe. Route 68. Follow the R68 southwards towards Gingindlovu until the route crosses the Nyezane stream. From this point the battlefield is only 0.75 miles (1km) further on and is situated on the right. A battlefield sign and the name of the farm, Kia-Ora, mark the entrance. Take this turning off the main road and follow the signs to the cemetery, which is 100 yards along the track.

Distinguishing features
The only obvious feature of the battlefield is the prominent leaning pine tree next to the battlefield. This tree can easily be seen from both directions, and in early 2002 it was a good marker point. Sadly, so much has changed since the battle. The battlefield is located in sugar cane fields; however, the cemetery is usually well maintained. A reasonable view of the battlefield can be gained from the cemetery itself.

Points of interest
1. The cemetery. Colonel Northey's remains were taken to England for re-burial.
2. Fort Eshowe is 12 miles (20km) to the north along the R68.
3. The battlefield of Nyezane is 10 miles (16km) to the north along the R68 and is clearly visible to the north.
4. The battlefield memorial.

Chapter 17

Death of the Prince Imperial of France,
1 June 1879

Having lost the war with Prussia at the Battle of Sedan in 1870, Napoleon III was taken prisoner, while his wife, the Empress Eugénie, and their young son Louis, the Prince Imperial, fled to England under the protection of Queen Victoria. Napoleon was later exiled to England, where he died on 9 January 1873.

The young Prince Imperial developed a strong interest in military matters and completed his education by attending the Woolwich Royal Academy, where officers for the Royal Artillery and Royal Engineers completed their training. He graduated seventh out of thirty-four officer cadets in 1875. Apart from occasional military exercises, Louis then began to languish. Being a French national, he could not hold a British commission. He applied to Emperor Franz Josef to be able to join the Austrian Army, but was refused.

At the outbreak of the Anglo-Zulu War, the young prince applied to The Duke of Cambridge for permission to go to South Africa. Following the positive intervention of his mother and Queen Victoria, permission was granted, and the prince was allocated to Chelmsford's staff as a civilian observer, where Louis proved to be dangerously irresponsible. After several incidents, instructions were given by Lord Chelmsford to all senior officers to confine him to camp at Fort Whitehead. On 1 June 1879 Louis persuaded Colonel Harrison to allow him to accompany a mapping patrol to reconnoitre the following day's campsite. Lieutenant Carey of the quartermaster general's staff led the patrol of six troopers of Bettington's Horse, although for the initial part of the journey they were accompanied by Major Grenfell, a senior staff officer (he later became Field Marshal Lord Grenfell). The area of the proposed campsite was near the river beyond Itelezi Hill.

The party rode for 8 miles along the ridge towards the Ityotyozi Valley, where Major Grenfell left the party to report to his new post at Itelezi Hill. At noon, the reduced party halted on a hilltop overlooking the river. Less than a

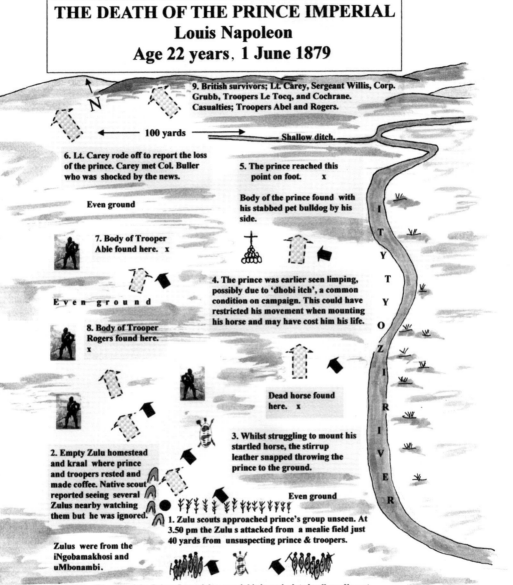

THE DEATH OF THE PRINCE IMPERIAL
Louis Napoleon
Age 22 years, 1 June 1879

9. British survivors; Lt. Carey, Sergeant Willis, Corp. Grubb, Troopers Le Tocq, and Cochrane. Casualties; Troopers Abel and Rogers.

N

← 100 yards →

Shallow ditch.

6. Lt. Carey rode off to report the loss of the prince. Carey met Col. Buller who was shocked by the news.

5. The prince reached this point on foot.   x

Even ground

Body of the prince found with his stabbed pet bulldog by his side.

7. Body of Trooper Able found here. x

4. The prince was earlier seen limping, possibly due to 'dhobi itch', a common condition on campaign. This could have restricted his movement when mounting his horse and may have cost him his life.

E v e n   g r o u n d

8. Body of Trooper Rogers found here. x

Dead horse found here. x

3. Whilst struggling to mount his startled horse, the stirrup leather snapped throwing the prince to the ground.

2. Empty Zulu homestead and kraal where prince and troopers rested and made coffee. Native scout reported seeing several Zulus nearby watching them but he was ignored.

Even ground

1. Zulu scouts approached prince's group unseen. At 3.50 pm the Zulus attacked from a mealie field just 40 yards from unsuspecting prince & troopers.

Zulus were from the iNgobamakhosi and uMbonambi.

The site of the Prince Imperial memorial is in an isolated valley adjacent to the Ityotyozi River. (Jojosi River on modern road maps).

mile away, they observed a small Zulu homestead, apparently deserted, next to a field of tall, dried maize. Carey finished his map and the Prince Imperial gave orders for the whole party to descend into the valley to the Zulu huts, where they could obtain water from the nearby river and make coffee. As the party descended the hill, they were observed by a small Zulu scouting party, who began to approach the group under cover of the maize field.

Unaware of the approaching Zulus, the men off-saddled their horses, and, as the ashes in the fireplace were still hot, a native guard was posted and coffee was brewed. At about 3.30 pm, the guide appeared and waved his hand towards the mealie field. Corporal Grubb interpreted for the guide and informed the party that the guide had seen some Zulus in the maize field. Without any urgency, the prince gave the order for the men to gather and re-saddle their horses, but it took some ten minutes before they were ready. Carey mounted his horse as the prince gave the order to mount. At that moment, a volley of rifle fire crashed out from the maize field at a distance of only 30 yards, and then the Zulus charged. The horses reared and began to bolt with the riders desperately trying to mount. Troopers Abel and Rogers fell, severely wounded or dead.

Graves of Troopers Abel and Rogers, killed alongside the Prince Imperial.

Carey controlled his horse and pointed it away from the huts and fled at a gallop, closely followed by the remainder of the party – or so Carey thought. The prince tried to mount his horse by vaulting into the saddle, but the holster strap he grabbed snapped under the strain. He fell heavily to the ground and, although dazed, managed to regain his feet as the Zulus closed with him. He ran towards a dry gulley and faced the Zulus. He drew his revolver and fired several shots before a spear struck him in the thigh. The prince withdrew the spear to use as a weapon, but the Zulus overwhelmed him. He sustained seventeen assegai wounds, all to his front.

Two hours later, Carey found Buller and reported that the Prince Imperial was dead. The immediate effect on the British establishment and the public was dramatic – almost as dramatic as the news of the defeat at Isandlwana. The body of the prince was carefully transported to England for burial. Carey was court-martialled and sent back to England under escort to await the result, but the findings were never confirmed. The British press championed Carey as an innocent scapegoat, and he was released back to his own regiment, then serving in India. He died in 1883 while still serving in India. The *Army and Navy Gazette* reported his death rather ambiguously:

> Captain J. Carey 98th Regiment, of unfortunate history in Zululand, has, we regret to hear, died under mysterious circumstances in India, a victim of much persecution.

Interestingly, the prince's mother, Eugénie, was born María Kirkpatrick, then living in France, and later had an affair with George Villiers, 4th Earl of Clarendon and British Foreign Secretary. Eugénie was the result of the affair, and the girl was brought up by Villiers in Bath, England, where she was known as 'carrot top'. It was Villiers who, as Foreign Secretary, later successfully introduced her as an eligible young woman to Napoleon III in Paris.

Location
The site of the Prince Imperial memorial is in an isolated valley adjacent to the Ityotyozi River (Jojosi River on modern road maps).

How to find it
As this site is difficult to find, it would be worthwhile taking a guide.

From Dundee. Take the R68 eastwards
for a distance of 27 miles (45km) to the
town of Nqutu. In the centre of the town,
go straight on at the crossroads and take
the dirt road towards Maduladula and
Nondweni. You then have a choice of
two routes:

a. **Better road**. Stay on this road for
12 miles (20km) until reaching a
T-junction, turn left. From this
point, the Prince Imperial Memorial
is signposted. After 2 miles (3.2km),
take the next turn left towards
Esigodini, which is signposted to the
memorial. As the road crosses the
river, the memorial will be directly to
the front.

The Prince Imperial Memorial with British
graves behind.

The lonely memorial of the Prince Imperial and British graves.

b. **Rough road**. After about 3 miles (5km), you will see power pylons parallel to the road. At this point there is an unsigned dirt road to the left. Follow this route for about 5 miles (8km). It crosses two streams before reaching the river. As the road crosses the river, the memorial is directly to the left front.

Distinguishing features

From about 1 mile away, it is possible to see an isolated clump of trees next to six Zulu huts. In late 2022 a visitors' car park was built.

Points of interest

1. The memorial is set within a low-walled cemetery. The stone that marks the actual memorial, known as the 'Victoria Cross', was erected by Major Stabb of the 32nd Regiment on the orders of Sir Garnet Wolseley. Curiously, a memo from Buckingham Palace, dated 28 May 1880 states, 'No orders have been given by the Queen to the Governor of any Colony to erect a cross to the late Prince Louis Napoleon'.
2. The graves of Troopers Abel and Rogers are behind the Prince Imperial memorial.

Recommendations

This is an isolated site that can only be reached by motor vehicle. There is a site warden who will produce the visitors' book for signature. Visitors to the site, due to its isolated position, are rare and, as such, will attract much curious attention and requests from the local children. Take a reliable and up-to-date local road map or GPS.

Chapter 18

Chelmsford's Advance on Ulundi, 3 June to 4 July 1879

Chelmsford commenced the second invasion of Zululand with two divisions on 3 June 1879, the day after the Prince Napoleon's body was found. Chelmsford led the 2nd Division to the north, and Major General Crealock's 1st Division advanced along the coast. Crealock was so badly hampered by the rivers blocking his route, and by his ponderous fortification of every bivouac, that his column became known as 'Crealock's crawlers'. While advancing towards Zungeni on 5 June, Buller skirmished with a 300 strong Zulu *impi* armed with captured Martini-Henry rifles. Under fire from the Zulus, Buller withdrew his force but lost one officer killed, and two men were injured. On 23 June, Lord Wolseley arrived in Durban to take over from Chelmsford, who avoided his signals, even Wolseley's direct order to Chelmsford not to engage the Zulus. By 2 July, Chelmsford's force was less than 5 miles from Ulundi, where they built Fort Nolela, sometimes mistakenly referred to as Fort Victoria.

Those at the fort had a clear view of Ulundi 4 miles distant across the river. Many of the troops were fresh recruits from England and were increasingly unnerved by the distant spectacle of the Zulus preparing for battle. There were several false alarms, and shots were fired by nervous guards observing Ulundi and the massing Zulus. In the evenings, the songs sung by the warriors as they went through their pre-battle rituals drifted across the river, further unsettling the waiting and anxious British troops. British watering parties went down to the river on the 2nd. They soon found themselves being sniped at, sending them scurrying back to the camp.

On 3 July, Buller was dispatched with a strong force of 500 mounted men towards Ulundi to select a position for the anticipated engagement. Buller's force was drawn from the 1st Squadron Mounted Infantry, the Frontier Light Horse, Transvaal Rangers, Baker's Horse, Natal Light Horse and the Edendale troop of the mounted black auxiliaries. Buller crossed the river in two parties:

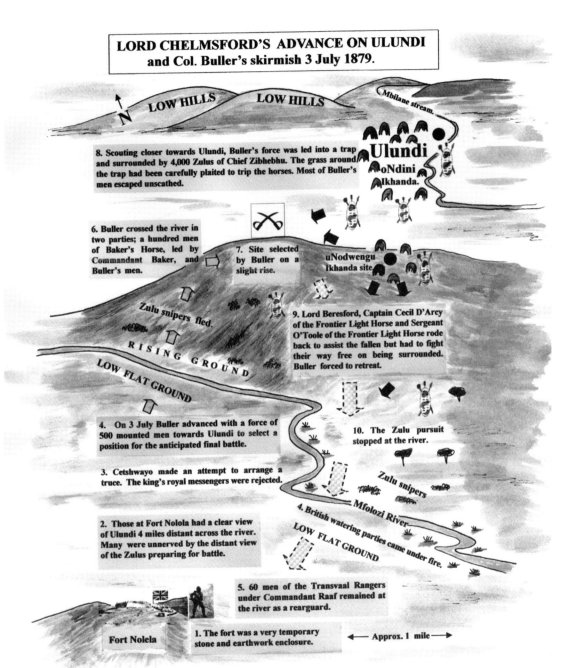

LORD CHELMSFORD'S ADVANCE ON ULUNDI
and Col. Buller's skirmish 3 July 1879.

N

LOW HILLS   LOW HILLS   Mbilane stream

Ulundi
oNdini
Ikhanda.

8. Scouting closer towards Ulundi, Buller's force was led into a trap and surrounded by 4,000 Zulus of Chief Zibhebhu. The grass around the trap had been carefully plaited to trip the horses. Most of Buller's men escaped unscathed.

6. Buller crossed the river in two parties; a hundred men of Baker's Horse, led by Commandant Baker, and Buller's men.

7. Site selected by Buller on a slight rise.

uNodwengu
Ikhanda site.

Zulu snipers fled.

RISING GROUND

LOW FLAT GROUND

9. Lord Beresford, Captain Cecil D'Arcy of the Frontier Light Horse and Sergeant O'Toole of the Frontier Light Horse rode back to assist the fallen but had to fight their way free on being surrounded. Buller forced to retreat.

4. On 3 July Buller advanced with a force of 500 mounted men towards Ulundi to select a position for the anticipated final battle.

10. The Zulu pursuit stopped at the river.

3. Cetshwayo made an attempt to arrange a truce. The king's royal messengers were rejected.

Zulu snipers

Mfolozi River

2. Those at Fort Nolola had a clear view of Ulundi 4 miles distant across the river. Many were unnerved by the distant view of the Zulus preparing for battle.

4. British watering parties came under fire.

LOW FLAT GROUND

5. 60 men of the Transvaal Rangers under Commandant Raaf remained at the river as a rearguard.

Fort Nolela

1. The fort was a very temporary stone and earthwork enclosure.

◄— Approx. 1 mile —►

Before the Battle of Ulundi. (*The Graphic*)

On the march to Ulundi. (*The Graphic*)

100 men of Baker's Horse, commanded by Commandant F.J. Baker and Buller's men who crossed the river at the old trader's drift directly below the British camp. Buller quickly identified a perfect area to defend on a slight rise in clear sight of Ulundi, just 2 miles distant.

Scouting closer towards Ulundi, Buller's force was uncharacteristically led into a trap near the Mbilane stream and surrounded by 4,000 Zulus of Chief Zibhebhu, the uMxapho, who opened heavy fire. Zulus were concealed in the long grass alongside the stream. The grass around the trap had been carefully plaited to trip the horses, and a number of Buller's riders were wounded and several unhorsed from their mounts. Most of his men escaped unscathed. Trooper Pearce of the Frontier Light Horse and Trooper Peacock of the Natal Light Horse were shot and killed outright. Trooper Raubenheim fell and was quickly killed, and the horse ridden by Sergeant Fitzmaurice 1/24th was hit, and rolled over, fatally trapping its rider. Lord Beresford, Captain Cecil D'Arcy and Sergeant O'Toole of the FLH rode back to assist the fallen but had to fight their way free on being surrounded. Buller was driven from the field and lost four men killed. The Zulu pursuit stopped at the river, where the warriors traded shots with the infantry, and the sixty men of the Transvaal Rangers under Commandant Raaf positioned at the river as a rearguard. The VC was awarded to Beresford, D'Arcy and O'Toole, while Sergeant Major Simeon Kambula of the Edendale Troop was awarded the DCM.

Earlier that evening, and seeing defeat staring him in the face, King Cetshwayo made an attempt to arrange a truce. The king's royal messengers, Nkisimane and Mfunzi, went to the British bearing the sword of the Prince Imperial in an act of truce, but they were rejected by the supremely confident Chelmsford anticipating the all-important final victory.

Chapter 19

Ulundi, 4 July 1879

This battle marks the final military defeat of the Zulu army. Chelmsford re-commenced the second invasion of Zululand on 3 June 1879, one day after the Prince Napoleon's body was found. Chelmsford's replacement, General Sir Garnett Wolseley, telegraphed to Chelmsford:

> Concentrate your forces immediately, undertake no operations and flash back your moves. Astonished at not hearing from you.

Chelmsford merely acknowledged receipt of the message.

At 6.00 am on the morning of 4 July 1879, the British set off towards Ulundi from their overnight position around Fort Nolela. They crossed the wide but shallow White Mfolozi River unopposed, and then, in a tightly packed column, moved towards the previously reconnoitred small rise in the middle of the Mahlabathini Plain. It was obvious to Chelmsford that the Zulus were reluctant to fight, but, by advancing his column towards King Cetshwayo's royal homestead, he successfully provoked the token battle he so desperately sought to save his reputation. With the King's homestead in view less than 3 miles distant, the Zulu regiments began to form up in opposition to the advancing column. As the British gained the high ground previously reconnoitred by Buller, Chelmsford ordered the 'form square', which the column did, turning to face the advancing Zulus and settling down to await the Zulu attack. Although now amassed and facing the British, the Zulus continued to show a reluctance to fight, so at 8.20 am Buller and his mounted troops moved out of the square to provoke the front Zulu ranks with several volleys of gunfire. In response, the Zulus charged and Buller withdrew into the square.

At about 9.00 am the Zulu warriors, already distressed by previous losses, were disorganized in their attacks, which soon faltered under the combined fire from Martini-Henry volleys, the Royal Artillery's 7- and 9-pounder guns and from two Gatling guns. Although the Zulus once managed to get to within

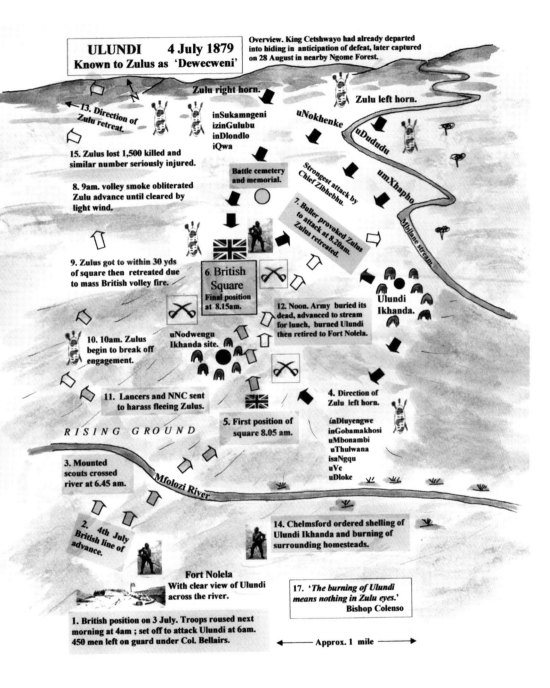

The Battle of Ulundi. (*The Graphic*)

30 yards of the British line, they could not sustain their assault. The Zulu chiefs and their reserves watched the attack falter and, disheartened, began to leave the battlefield, which added to the growing confusion among the attacking front line Zulu warriors. With the Zulu attack contained, Chelmsford again ordered Buller and his mounted troops out of the square, along with the 17th Lancers, to harass the retreating Zulus. The rout continued for another two hours and for several miles in all directions until the fleeing Zulus had either escaped or been killed.

After the battle, the Royal Artillery shelled Cetshwayo's homestead before it was sacked and burned. It was Chelmsford's final aggressive act of the war. Contrary to expectations, there was, according to one officer, 'no treasure worth looting'. With Chelmsford's fighting square still intact, orders were given for the column's three dead officers and ten men to be buried and the seventy casualties tended to. The column then marched on for another 0.5 miles to the Mbilane stream. After eating a midday meal, the column retraced its steps back to the camp near the White Mfolozi River. The final battle of the Anglo-

Zulu War had lasted just 40 minutes. Bishop Colenso was more acerbic in his observations on the defeat of the Zulus; he wrote, 'the battle of Ulundi was not important to the Zulus'.

On 24 July, as the last of Chelmsford's force were approaching Natal, the abaQulusi Zulus again sought to attack the British; King Cetshwayo refused them permission. Cetshwayo remained a fugitive until he was finally captured on 28 August 1879. He was held a prisoner of the British until 1883, when, at the request of Queen Victoria, he was returned to Zululand.

Participants

The total force amounted to 4,132 white troops and 1,009 black troops.

Imperial: Lieutenant General Lord Chelmsford, with the 2nd Division commanded by Major General Newdigate, commanding the column. The Flying Column (formally the Northern Column) was commanded by Brigadier General Sir Evelyn Wood. The 2nd Division included units of the 1st King's Dragoon Guards, the 17th (Duke of Cambridge's Own) Lancers, Royal Artillery, Royal Engineers, the 2/21st Royal Scots Fusiliers, the 94th Regiment and the 58th (Rutlandshire) Regiment. The Flying Column included units from the Royal Artillery, Royal Engineers, 1/13th Light Infantry, the 80th Regiment, the 90th Light Infantry, the Army Medical Department, Hospital Corps, Imperial Mounted Infantry and the Army Staff Corps.

Colonial: 2nd Battalion of the NNC, Shepstone's Horse, Bettington's Horse, Wood's Irregulars, Natal Pioneers, Transvaal Rangers, Frontier Light Horse, Baker's Horse, Natal Light Horse and the Natal Native Horse.

On the day of the battle, the newly reconstituted 1/24th Regiment was held in reserve, two companies at Fort Marshall and five companies at Fort Nolela. Chelmsford was fully aware that they were 24th Regiment but in name only, as fresh and inexperienced recruit replacements drawn from thirteen home-based regiments.

Zulu: The total Zulu force was estimated at 20,000 warriors and consisted of elements of various *amabutho* under the command of Ziwedu, Cetshwayo's brother. He was supported by three battle-experienced *indunas*, Mnyamana

Buthelezi (the Zulu prime minister), Prince Dabulamanzi (commanded at Rorke's Drift) and Ntshingwayo Khoza (commanded at Isandlwana).

Casualties

Column: 2 officers and 10 men were killed, with 1 officer and 69 men wounded.

Zulu: Not less than 1,450 dead warriors were found around the battlefield. Most of these would have been killed during the rout.

It was the victory that Chelmsford so desperately sought and, with the battle won, the British began to withdraw from Zululand.

Location

Route 1. From Durban. Take either the R102 to Gingindlovu or the new N2 motorway north from Durban. Take the first exit to Eshowe and Gingindlovu, which brings one onto the route R102. Follow the signs to Gingindlovu and Eshowe. On approaching the town of Gingindlovu, remain on the R102 avoiding the town centre. Within a few hundred yards, take the left fork to Eshowe, the R66. Follow this road for a further 72 miles (120km), passing through Eshowe and Melmoth until the high plain overlooking Ulundi is reached. Take the obvious right-hand turn off the R66 towards Ulundi. Descending from the high plateau, the road crosses the White Mfolozi River, and on entering the outskirts of Ulundi, take the right-hand turn that is signposted to Mangosuthu Buthelezi Airport and to the battlefield. Stay on this road for half a mile and the battlefield will appear on the left-hand side of the road. The domed building in the middle of the site indicates the battlefield. The British cemetery is at the eastern end of the fenced area.

Route 2. From Isandlwana or Rorke's Drift. Route 68. On joining the R68, head east towards Babanango, 40 miles (61km), and Melmoth, a further 25 miles (42km). On reaching the junction with the R66 as you approach Melmoth, take the left turn towards Ulundi. The route leads to the high plain overlooking Ulundi. Once this is reached, take the obvious right-hand turn off the high ground towards Ulundi. Descending down a long hill, the road crosses the White Mfolozi River and, on entering the outskirts of Ulundi, take the right-hand turn that is signposted to Mangosuthu Buthelezi Airport and to the battlefield. Stay on this road for half a mile, and the battlefield will appear on the left-hand side of the road. The battlefield can easily be identified by the domed building in the middle of the site. The British cemetery is at the eastern end of the fenced area.

Recommendations

Walk around the whole battlefield and visit the cemetery at the far end. The battlefield is very compact. After visiting the battlefield, continue for 1 mile (1.6km) further along the dirt road, crossing the Mbilane stream, until you come to the Zulu Cultural Museum. Enter the museum compound with its large car park; tickets can be obtained from the orientation centre just inside the entrance gate. On the north side of the museum, visitors can walk round the original site of King Cetshwayo's homestead. The site of the massacre of Piet Retief and his men is only 12miles (20km) distant – see Mgungundhlovu.

Points of interest

1. The battlefield memorial. The protected area is on the approximate location of Chelmsford's square.
2. The route taken by Chelmsford's square.
3. The British cemetery. This is at the far end of the battlefield square.
4. The Ulundi Museum.
5. The original site of King Cetshwayo's royal homestead. Parts of it have been reconstructed in the original style.
6. The site where the British column advanced to and had lunch before returning to Fort Nolela.
7. Where Buller's force was ambushed on 3 July, the day before the battle.
8. Fort Nolela overlooking the White Mfolozi River.

Chapter 20

The British Withdrawal from Zululand after 4 July 1879

The war was over. It had cost the British 76 officers and 1,007 men killed, plus a similar number of black Natal auxiliaries. A further 17 officers and 330 men had died of disease, and 99 officers and 1,286 men were invalided from the campaign. It fell to Chelmsford's successor, Sir Garnet Wolseley, to oversee and then supervise the settlement of the defeated Zulus.

At Ulundi there was no clearing of the battlefield. For many weeks, only deserted and smouldering villages evidenced the once thriving heart of the Zulu nation. The dead bodies of slain Zulus remained where they had fallen, and these were left to the predators or to rot and shrivel in the sun. The British roughly estimated that not less than 1,500 Zulus had died in the battle for Ulundi, while Buller suggested that his mounted men increased the death toll by yet another 500 during the far-ranging Zulu rout. Exact figures for Zulu losses during the war are impossible to assess. They certainly lost 10,000 warriors killed in action, and conservative estimates suggest a similar number probably died from their injuries.

But the main prize for Wolseley, King Cetshwayo, was still missing, although it could only be a matter of time before he was found and captured. With the king still at large, and with so many bands of Zulus left wandering about the country, the potential for a resumption of conflict, albeit on a small scale, nevertheless continued to smoulder. Indeed, neither the loss of the Battle for Ulundi nor the burning of the king's capital was particularly significant to the Zulus. Ulundi could have been rebuilt quickly, and the northern abaQulusi Zulus remained bitterly opposed to any suggestion of surrender. As for Chelmsford, he had no intention of chasing after King Cetshwayo. Capturing the king and restoring normality to Zululand would be thankless tasks that would occupy Wolseley, his recently arrived successor, for many weeks if not months. Chelmsford was fully aware that before Wolseley could report anything detrimental about him, he would already be back in London, with Ulundi being portrayed by his staff as a brilliant victory; the glory would be his to enjoy.

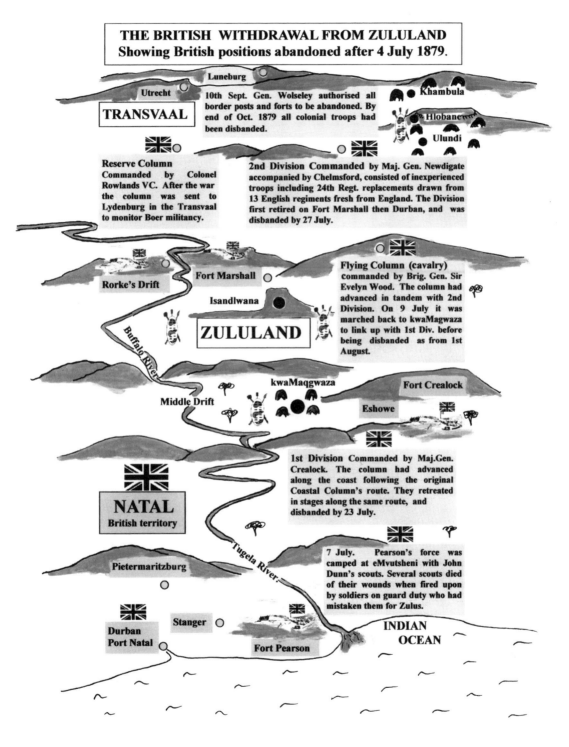

THE BRITISH WITHDRAWAL FROM ZULULAND
Showing British positions abandoned after 4 July 1879.

Luneburg

Utrecht

TRANSVAAL

10th Sept. Gen. Wolseley authorised all border posts and forts to be abandoned. By end of Oct. 1879 all colonial troops had been disbanded.

Khambula

Hlobane

Ulundi

Reserve Column Commanded by Colonel Rowlands VC. After the war the column was sent to Lydenburg in the Transvaal to monitor Boer militancy.

2nd Division Commanded by Maj. Gen. Newdigate accompanied by Chelmsford, consisted of inexperienced troops including 24th Regt. replacements drawn from 13 English regiments fresh from England. The Division first retired on Fort Marshall then Durban, and was disbanded by 27 July.

Rorke's Drift

Fort Marshall

Isandlwana

ZULULAND

Buffalo River

Flying Column (cavalry) commanded by Brig. Gen. Sir Evelyn Wood. The column had advanced in tandem with 2nd Division. On 9 July it was marched back to kwaMagwaza to link up with 1st Div. before being disbanded as from 1st August.

kwaMaqgwaza

Middle Drift

Fort Crealock

Eshowe

1st Division Commanded by Maj.Gen. Crealock. The column had advanced along the coast following the original Coastal Column's route. They retreated in stages along the same route, and disbanded by 23 July.

NATAL
British territory

Tugela River

7 July. Pearson's force was camped at eMvutsheni with John Dunn's scouts. Several scouts died of their wounds when fired upon by soldiers on guard duty who had mistaken them for Zulus.

Pietermaritzburg

Stanger

Durban
Port Natal

Fort Pearson

INDIAN
OCEAN

On 6 July, the column was struck by severe storms. The hail was fierce enough to kill hundreds of oxen, and numerous horses died while the soldiers took cover where they could. The abnormal conditions released a plague of snake-like worms into the British position; some were over 3ft long and an inch thick, which added to the troops' woe. The men were cheered with extra supplies of rum, and, on the 10th, the weather cleared.

On the return march to Natal, it was evident to the troops that the watching Zulus were still a formidable force, and they were greatly unnerved by them. Pearson's force was camped near the deserted mission station at eMvutsheni when they were joined by a number of John Dunn's followers. On the evening of 7 July, Dunn's black scouts were manning the outer camp picket when, in the early hours of darkness, a picket of the 91st Regiment mistakenly sounded the alarm. Dunn's men scurried back to the safety of the camp, only to stumble onto a line of waiting bayonets. Mistaken for Zulus, a number were seriously injured, and several died of their wounds, a repeat of the incident on 6 April at Fort Pearson.

On 24 August, Wolseley learned that the abaQulusi Zulus intended to resume opposing the remaining British. While he was considering this new threat, the fugitive king ordered all Zulus, including the abaQulusi, to surrender. The king knew that, otherwise, the war would have continued. Although the British presumed the war was over, they were still seriously engaged in operations to the north of the country. Peace would not reach the Ntombe River Zulus for another two months. The troops then began marching out of Zululand and left its people, particularly those whose wasted homes and livelihoods had the misfortune of being along the invasion route, to their fate.

Chelmsford returned to Cape Town, where he received an enthusiastic reception from the European population for whom Ulundi had eradicated the memories of earlier disasters. Wolseley later commented that 'since his [Chelmsford's] fight, he is all cock-a-hoop. Poor fellow, I can understand his feelings and am anxious to let him down easy'. Chelmsford sailed home on the RMS *German* in the company of Wood and Buller, his most effective and reliable commanders, although both had earlier confided to Wolseley that they objected strongly to Chelmsford's associating with them and thereby giving the impression that 'they were in the same boat and going home because the war was over'.

On 31 August, Cetshwayo was captured and brought by cart to Wolseley's camp overlooking the scarred remains of Ulundi. After Cetshwayo alighted from the cart, his terrified wives hung on to him, believing he was doomed to immediate execution. He strode in with the aid of his long stick, with a proud and dignified air and grace, looking every inch the warrior king. He wore his grand *umutcha* of leopard skin and tails, with lion's teeth and claw charms round his neck. Well over 6ft, fat but not corpulent, with a stern air to him, he looked as he was, a proud ruler. Arrogant as ever, and not to be outdone, Wolseley declined to meet with the king, merely sending him a message that he would remain a captive of the British. At that, the king's resolve left him, and he was seen to dejectedly crumple. After that, the royal party was driven in a mule wagon to the coast via kwaMagwaza and St Paul's. In charge of the party were Lieutenants Poole and Harford, with a mounted escort. From the coast, he was embarked onto the steamer, *Natal*, which took him into exile at the castle at Cape Town.

Wolseley now assumed command from Chelmsford, who returned to England. Over the next few weeks, the British eliminated what little resistance remained in Zululand. On 28 August, King Cetshwayo was captured by British soldiers from the 1st King's Dragoon Guards in the Ngome Forest and taken to Port Durnford, where he was put on a boat for Cape Town.

Once the remaining groups of Zulus heard that the king had been captured, most sought to make peace. The remnants under Chief Manyanyoba also tried to give themselves up, but their attempt to surrender coincided with an unnecessary order from Wolseley to a local commander, The Honourable Colonel Villiers, that he should 'clear Manyanyoba out', and on Villiers' orders, troops under Colonel Black marched out to Manyanyoba's stronghold overlooking the Ntombe River, where a group of warriors promptly surrendered. The troops then advanced towards a number of caves where the remaining warriors, women, children and animals were hiding. Unfortunately, one of the warriors in a cave inadvertently discharged his rifle, whereupon the warriors who had just surrendered were immediately slaughtered by their guards, who suspected a trap. The surrender of Manyanyoba and his people came to a halt, and the troops marched back to camp. On 5 September, the troops returned to deal with Manyanyoba and attempted to smoke the Zulus from their caves, without success. On 8 September, the troops returned and destroyed the caves with dynamite, notwithstanding that they were still sheltering many Zulus. On 22 September, Manyanyoba, unprepared to take further losses, surrendered to the British. He and his surviving followers were escorted to the Batshe Valley, near Rorke's Drift, where they sought to settle.

Meanwhile, the Zulu war heralded the end of confederation that had contributed to the war in the first place and now gave the increasingly antagonistic Boers the freedom to encroach further into Zululand. The British government, worried by the cost of Frere's policies, refused to annex Zululand, and Wolseley was left to devise a suitable settlement. He divided Zululand among thirteen newly appointed chiefs, some of whom had been overtly sympathetic to the British cause while others were openly hostile to the Cetshwayo's Royal House.

Zululand was effectively divided into thirteen independent 'chiefdoms', each ruled by a Zulu chief selected and appointed by the British, each chief to have command under the overall supervision of a British resident. The intention was to divide the Zulu people against themselves and block any individual, of royal birth or otherwise, from ever reuniting the Zulus and prevent them uniting to threaten British interests. The 1879 settlement was deliberately designed to set Zulu against Zulu, the new borders of the country and the boundaries of the chiefdoms indiscriminately cutting across both the social and political groupings that had developed during the previous fifty years. Melmoth Osborn, an ex-naval officer, was appointed as the British Resident Administrator, but the position lacked any real administrative or legislative authority, only diplomatic duties.

The chiefs were to abolish the formal Zulu military system and not obstruct any of their people who might wish to work in neighbouring territories. This requirement was especially destructive as it encouraged the migration of male Zulus to the British controlled gold and diamond fields located to the north and west, and the agricultural enterprises in the south. The Zulus were forbidden to import firearms or become involved in any form of trade that did not reach them through British-controlled Natal or the Transvaal. Capital punishment without trial was forbidden; land could not be sold or purchased without British permission, and they were to keep the peace and apply the law according to the 'ancient laws and customs' of their people, so long as these laws did not offend the sensitivities of the British administrator. This policy unleashed powerful destructive forces within the kingdom; it resulted in a decade of violence and civil war that more effectively destroyed the basis of Zulu royal power than the British invasion.

As a result of these unreasonable provisions, Zululand was plunged into a state of civil war as Zulu fought against Zulu, with more Zulu blood spilled in the following period than in 1879.

With regard to Cetshwayo's relatives, Wolseley gave instructions that members of the royal house should abandon their homes and move into Dunn's territory, an order that was simply ignored. Wolseley further instructed the appointed chiefs to collect royal cattle and firearms and deliver them to the Resident Administrator. Of all Wolseley's dictums, this one most irritated the Zulus; after all, cattle were virtually the currency of the Zulu economy. Both directly and indirectly, Cetshwayo owned most of Zululand's cattle, which made him the wealthiest man in the kingdom. His royal herds were easily recognized by their whiteness as belonging to the King, and, due to their large numbers, they were distributed among many royal households. Wolseley's instructions merely gave those newly appointed chiefs, who felt sufficiently confident, a golden opportunity to seize the King's cattle and plunder from those Zulus who had previously been loyal to Cetshwayo.

From Cape Town, King Cetshwayo repeatedly petitioned Sir Hercules Robinson to request Queen Victoria to grant him an audience seeking to be allowed to return to Zululand. He finally arrived in England in August 1882 and was later presented to Queen Victoria at Osborne House on the Isle of Wight. Partly as a result of this meeting, steps were taken to return Cetshwayo to Zululand as King of the Zulus. Worried that the escalating violence in Zululand might still spill over into Natal, the government eventually agreed to restore Cetshwayo to part of his old territory, but with severe constraints. He returned to Zululand in February 1883, but during his absence, his supporters had quarrelled with his kinsman, Zibhebhu kaMaphitha, who had been one of the most daring commanders in 1879 but had then accepted a post in Wolseley's settlement. Inevitably, a protracted civil war broke out, and in July 1883, Zibhebhu launched a surprise attack on Cetshwayo's rebuilt Ulundi homestead. The royalists were heavily defeated, and over sixty of the most important chiefs loyal to Cetshwayo were killed. These included Ntshingwayo, who had commanded at Isandlwana and Khambula, and Sihayo, whose sons' actions had precipitated the British ultimatum.

King Cetshwayo was wounded in the fighting and took refuge with the British Resident Administrator at Eshowe, attended by his own close circle of advisors. A broken soul, he died in February 1884, probably the victim of poison administered by his own people. He was buried in a remote area near the Mome Gorge, the last refuge of the Zulus, where the last great struggle of the infamous Bambata uprising took place in 1906. His son, King Dinuzulu, desperately attempted to salvage the royalist cause. Sporadic violence continued for four more years, during which Dinuzulu secured Boer help to defeat Zibhebhu, but costing the lives of a number of the prominent supporters of the old order. In 1884 the Boers murdered Prince Dabulamanzi, who had commanded at Rorke's Drift. Dinuzulu, continually harassed by the Colonial authorities, and was eventually goaded into leading armed resistance against the British in 1888. He was defeated, and sent into exile on St Helena.

The traditions of the Zulu *amabutho* continued to shape the defiant attitudes of the Zulus towards Colonial authority well into the twentieth century. In 1906, Africans living in Natal took up arms to protest at the harsh levels of taxation imposed upon them. One of the few Zulu chiefs to openly support them was Mehlokazulu kaSihayo. Mehlokazulu had served throughout the Anglo-Zulu War as an officer in the iNgobamakhosi Regiment, and, in 1906, he threw in his lot with the rebel leader Bambatha. But the balance of power had swung even more in favour of the Europeans, and the rebel army was crushed at the Battle of Mome Gorge, where both Bambatha and Mehlokazulu were killed.

The Anglo-Zulu War of 1879 left many marks on the Zululand landscape. The British dead lay unburied at Isandlwana for nearly four months until the first patrols attempted to bury them. Due to the hard terrain and violent rain storms the first hasty burials were so ineffective that several further visits were necessary before the end of 1879, and thorough interments were not completed until 1884. The whitewashed cairns so characteristic of the battlefield today mark the approximate positions of the British mass graves. The enormous amount of debris scattered across the veldt during the Zulu looting of the camp continued to surface well into the twentieth century, attracting in more recent time the unwelcome attention of souvenir hunters.

The Anglo-Zulu War heralded the end of Britain's policy of confederation that had contributed to the war in the first place. The British government, worried by the cost of Frere's policies, refused to annex Zululand. Chelmsford, favourite of Queen Victoria, returned to England as the victor of Ulundi rather than the vanquished of Isandlwana. He was presented with a number of prestigious honours, but never allowed to command British troops in the field. In 1905 he died during a billiards match at his club in London. Chard and Bromhead enjoyed considerable fame as heroes of Rorke's Drift throughout their lives; Bromhead died in India in 1891 and Chard in England in 1897. Colour Sergeant Bourne, who had won the DCM during the battle, lived to see the fall of Hitler's Germany and died in 1945.

Zululand remained in turmoil until 1906 when the Zulu Rebellion took place.

Chapter 21

The British Attack against King Sekhukhune at Tsate, 28 November 1879

Having defeated the Zulus, Wolseley marched out of Zululand. Ever ready to embrace his next challenge, he headed for Pretoria, capital of the old Transvaal Republic, to quell an upsurge in republican sentiment amongst Boers not reconciled to the British annexation of 1877. Wolseley was convinced their agitation would melt away when faced with the sight of British troops fresh from their successes in Zululand. En route was Sekhukhuneland.

Although the British had defeated the Zulus, the same tensions which had provoked the war in Zululand were still bearing down upon the Pedi nation, ruled by King Sekhukhune. He had proved to be an able and determined ruler who was fiercely opposed to further European settlement. As recently as 1878, his warriors had seen off a full-scale British expedition against them, led by Colonel Rowlands VC.

But now Wolseley was in charge. Still nurturing his resentment for having missed the opportunity of defeating the Zulus at Ulundi, the equally glittering prize of defeating King Sekhukhune was still his for the taking, especially as Chelmsford had failed to remove him. Unaffected by the Zulu campaign, King Cetshwayo was still at large, and earlier British attempts to subdue him had already cost the British government too much. Wolseley would take much satisfaction in defeating the rebellious king.

On 18 October, Wolseley reached Standerton. He wrote, 'the news from Sikekhuni's country is very serious, Sikekhuni will fight'. Adding, no doubt tongue-in-cheek, 'this is a great bore for me'. Wolseley had hoped the utter humiliation vented upon Cetshwayo might have reduced Sekhukhune into submission. Instead, the Pedi were preparing for a last-ditch stand for fear the Zulus' fate might befall them.

In mid-October, Wolseley concentrated all available troops in the Transvaal and moved his headquarters to Middleburg. His principle attack column was

THE BRITISH EXPEDITION AGAINST KING SEKUKHUNE TSATE, 28 November 1879.

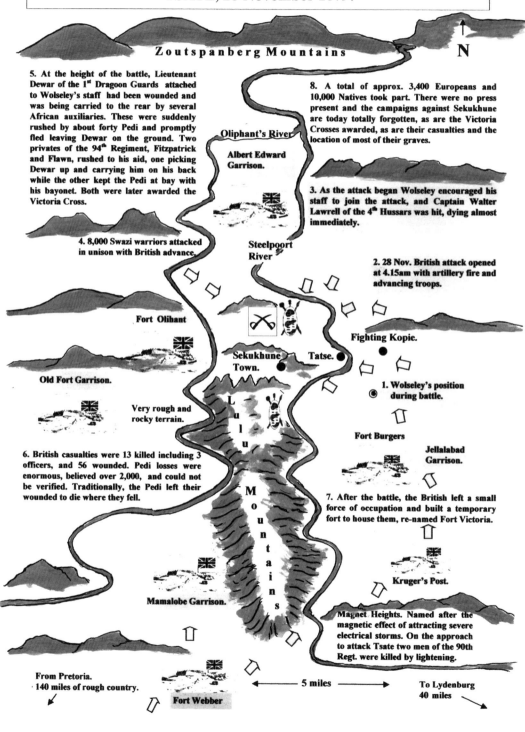

Zoutspanberg Mountains

N

5. At the height of the battle, Lieutenant Dewar of the 1st Dragoon Guards attached to Wolseley's staff had been wounded and was being carried to the rear by several African auxiliaries. These were suddenly rushed by about forty Pedi and promptly fled leaving Dewar on the ground. Two privates of the 94th Regiment, Fitzpatrick and Flawn, rushed to his aid, one picking Dewar up and carrying him on his back while the other kept the Pedi at bay with his bayonet. Both were later awarded the Victoria Cross.

Oliphant's River

Albert Edward Garrison.

8. A total of approx. 3,400 Europeans and 10,000 Natives took part. There were no press present and the campaigns against Sekukhune are today totally forgotten, as are the Victoria Crosses awarded, as are their casualties and the location of most of their graves.

4. 8,000 Swazi warriors attacked in unison with British advance.

Steelpoort River

3. As the attack began Wolseley encouraged his staff to join the attack, and Captain Walter Lawrell of the 4th Hussars was hit, dying almost immediately.

2. 28 Nov. British attack opened at 4.15am with artillery fire and advancing troops.

Fort Olihant

Fighting Kopie.

Old Fort Garrison.

Sekukhune Town.

Tatse.

1. Wolseley's position during battle.

Very rough and rocky terrain.

Lulu Mountains

Fort Burgers

Jellalabad Garrison.

6. British casualties were 13 killed including 3 officers, and 56 wounded. Pedi losses were enormous, believed over 2,000, and could not be verified. Traditionally, the Pedi left their wounded to die where they fell.

7. After the battle, the British left a small force of occupation and built a temporary fort to house them, re-named Fort Victoria.

Kruger's Post.

Mamalobe Garrison.

Magnet Heights. Named after the magnetic effect of attracting severe electrical storms. On the approach to attack Tsate two men of the 90th Regt. were killed by lightening.

From Pretoria. 140 miles of rough country.

5 miles

To Lydenburg 40 miles

Fort Webber

placed under Lieutenant Colonel Baker-Russell. All had recent experience in the Zulu campaign and most were present at the Battle of Ulundi. Among his mounted irregular troops was the even more experienced FLH. While the NNC had been disbanded at the end of the Zulu campaign, Wolseley set about raising new native auxiliary forces from the various African groups in the Transvaal. The Swazis also offered 10,000 magnificently attired warriors in return for the promise that they could keep any Pedi cattle they could plunder and share whatever fine was levied against the Pedi people. A few Swazis had rifles, but the majority of the warriors were armed with assegais. They marched over 150 miles from the Swazi king's royal homestead and drilled on the way.

Wolseley and his staff approached the new campaign with typical energy and efficiency, arriving at Fort Webber on 28 October to find that, owing to transport difficulties, supplies were behind schedule and inadequate. Wolseley personally set about rectifying this state of affairs with great energy and then reconnoitred the area ahead to get some idea of the nature of the objective and any terrain problems. The plan was to advance up the course of the Oliphants River and swing round north of the Pedi base at Tsate. Then, following a valley which ran southwards along the eastern edge of the Leolu Mountains, he planned to advance directly towards his objective of Tsate. The Swazis, meanwhile, would advance directly from Swaziland, to the south-east, and mount a direct attack on Tsate in the rear.

On 23 November, Wolseley advanced. He was not opposed, but King Sekhukhune had meanwhile gathered his fighting men, ready to make a determined stand in front of his capital. There are few accurate assessments of their numbers, but there were probably less than 10,000 men. They were, however, heavily armed with obsolete but poor quality weapons, which represented the profits of their several years involvement in the diamond industry. Their position was a strong one. Tsate was a large settlement of about 3,000 huts nestled at the foot of a horse-shoe of rocky hills and protected by an isolated outcrop known to the Boers as the 'fighting *kopje*', after their earlier failed campaign. This unusual feature lay between the township and the valley beyond, directly in the line of Wolseley's advance. It is a jumble of volcanic rock, no more than 300ft long, 200ft across and 150ft high, but it was a natural fortress, with deep fissures, crevices and caves hidden among the piled-up boulders, that the Pedi had carefully reinforced with rows of stone walls.

British attack against King Sekhukhune. (*Courtesy of Ian Knight*)

As was invariably the case with campaigning in Africa, the terrain was difficult, and violent rain and hail storms harassed the advancing column until the narrow old Boer track, overgrown with dense bush, became almost impassable. The wagons stuck in the mud, and the cracking of the whips overlaid by the thunder and lightning must have reminded many of the advance on Isandlwana or the withdrawal from Ulundi. Men of the 21st and the 94th Regiments who had been under arms for 24 hours arrived, soaked and dispirited, stumbling into the new camp site in the early hours of the 27 November. Everything was now in place for the final assault on Sekhukhune's fortress base.

After viewing the *koppie* from a safe distance, Wolseley selected a suitable camp-site and a position for the guns. His plan of attack was to first strike the mountain with the irregulars and auxiliaries who would advance past the *koppie* on either side to attack the Tsate township. This frontal attack was largely a feint, for Wolseley had instructed the Swazis to approach over the hills from behind the township and storm it, hopefully taking the defenders in their rear and by surprise. Meanwhile the *koppie* would be shelled and contained by the regular troops. Once the township defenders had been destroyed or driven off, the isolated rock fortress would then be assaulted from all sides. But unbeknown

to the attackers, there were numerous deep caves above the township to which
the Pedi were prepared to move if driven from their defensive positions.
The British were also unaware that Sekhukhune and his retinue had already
retreated to one of these caves to watch and control the battle.

Well before dawn on the morning of 28 November, the men were silently
roused, the tents were struck, and without any loud orders, the men formed up
in front of the camp. The column then moved forward swiftly across the valley
with sufficient moonlight to enable them to see the mountain. Wolseley and
his staff seated themselves under a tree to watch the attack, and, at the first
glimmer of dawn, a shell was fired into the 'Fighting Koppie', which instantly
became alive with the defenders firing and yelling to alert the sleeping Pedi in
the town and on the hillside.

While the infantry in the centre did no more than line up in support of the
guns, the irregulars and auxiliaries began their attack on the town, from where,
on both sides, they were met at first by strong resistance from Pedi defenders
concealed in rifle-pits, an unheard of tactic for natives and one which took the
advancing British troops by surprise. The Pedi were also positioned behind
walls in front of the huts, but these were soon outflanked and the defenders
rapidly retired to the slopes above the settlement. On both sides, the fighting
became a sporadic struggle to clear these slopes while the artillery continued to
shell the isolated 'fighting *kopje*'.

Once they realized the British were in earnest, the Swazi regiments moved
quickly up the heights behind the town, and at about 6.00 am the first line
of their distinctive shields appeared across the summit in the early-morning
light. They then swept down the hillside towards the battle, inflicting a great
massacre on the fleeing Pedi. The Volunteers and the Swazis met halfway up
the mountain, where the Pedi dead lay everywhere.

Clumps of warriors were still concealed among the rocks on the slopes, and
there were stiff flurries of hand-to-hand fighting as the Swazis cleared the
boulders. Many Pedi women and children were still hiding in the caves, and
a great crowd of them was soon driven out running towards the town, which
added to the chaos. By about 9.30 am, a great cloud of smoke began to billow
up as the huts were set alight; Tsate was in the hands of the invaders. The loss
of life among the Pedi, both fighting men and non-combatants, had been heavy.

Only the 'fighting *kopje*' resisted. With the town taken, the troops were now
able to surround the *koppie* on all sides, and Wolseley gave the order for it to

be taken by storm. The regulars, unused to this type of warfare, were clumsy and vulnerable, but it was a type of fighting at which the Swazi excelled. They jumped casually from boulder, to boulder spearing any Pedi they found hiding. An hour later the attackers had completely over-run the *kopje*.

But there remained a serious problem; hundreds of Pedi men, women and children refused to surrender and were still hidden among the caves, firing on anyone who approached them. Wolseley ordered parties from the Royal Engineers to blow up some of the caves with gun-cotton, a tactic which had earlier worked well at Ntombe. But the Pedi were familiar from their mining days with the concept of explosives; they would run forward and cut the fuses before the charges could explode.

Then an impressive thunderstorm developed. Clouds blotted out the sky so that an inky blackness descended over the battlefield only to be rent with sudden lightning flashes and deafening peals of thunder. The Pedi warriors still trapped on the *kopje* spotted their chance. The soldiers being deployed as a cordon were clearly disorientated and distracted by the storm, so hundreds of Pedi made a rush at the nearest part of the line, bounding over the boulders, and in some cases leaping clear over the heads of the soldiers. Despite the break-out, there were still hundreds of men and women hiding among the crevices. When they refused to surrender, the troops and Swazis were all withdrawn, and a cordon of men was placed in a trench around the *koppie* with the object of starving them out. The remainder of the force retired to camp at about 1.00 pm.

Altogether, three officers and ten Europeans had been killed, and another thirty wounded. The dead were buried close to the camp. The loss among the African auxiliaries was not properly recorded, although some assumed that the Pedi losses ran to thousands. The survivors of the 'fighting *kopje*' then began to surrender. The hill was covered with unburied dead from the fighting and a heavy stench of death soon hung in the air. Many Pedi, weakened by wounds and lack of water and food, never emerged from their hiding places, and, after the last surrenders, the Royal Engineers were again ordered to dynamite the most conspicuous of the caves.

A party of irregulars and Swazis were sent out to hunt for King Sekhukhune, and on the morning of 2 December he was discovered hiding in a cave. The Swazis laid siege to the entrance, but the king refused to come out until a party of Ferreira's Horse arrived. They dismissed the Swazis and assured the king he would be safe. When, at last, the king emerged, he was taken under guard to Wolseley's camp, and for the second time in a few short months, Wolseley witnessed the sight of a once-proud and powerful African monarch brought before him a prisoner.

With the king's power-base now destroyed, Wolseley dismissed his troops. The Swazi were sent home, driving before them herds of Pedi cattle as a reward for their decisive role in the attack. A few of the irregulars were left to hold forts around Sekhukhuneland. The regular 94th Regiment returned to their base at Lydenburg, while the rest, with Wolseley and his staff, set off for Pretoria, arriving there on 9 December to find a large crowd turned out to watch the captured king arrive in town aboard a wagon.

At the end of March, Wolseley left the Transvaal, his job there done, and at the beginning of April he embarked at Durban for home. Eight months later, the Boers in the Transvaal rose in deadly revolt. The short British campaigns to defeat Sekhukhune cost the British Exchequer a comparative fortune, a total of £383,000 compared with the Anglo-Zulu War, which had amounted to £5,230,323.

Wolseley's main column was as follows:
Six companies of the 2nd Battalion, 21st (Royal Scots Fusiliers) Regiment
Six companies of the 2nd Battalion, 94th (Connaught Rangers) Regiment
Detachments of the 2nd Battalion, 80th (Staffordshire Volunteers) Regiment
Ferreira's Horse
Border Horse
Transvaal Mounted Rifles
Two squadrons of coloured mounted men
Four RA mountain guns
Royal Engineers
Rustenburg Contingent (*Bantu* levies)
Zoutpansberg Contingent (*Bantu* levies)

During the night of 13 August 1882, at a place called Manoge, King Sekhukhune was murdered by his half-brother, Mampuru, who claimed that he was the lawful king and that Sekhukhune had usurped the throne on 21 September 1861 when their father, Sekwati, died.

Location

This region is mainly grassland and was inhabited traditionally by the Bapedi in an area stretching across central and northern Transvaal. Sekhukhuneland is in the Transvaal to the north of Zululand and just 120 miles east of Pretoria and north-west of the Swazi kingdom and lies in present-day Limpopo and Mpumalanga provinces, between the Olifants River (Lepelle) and its tributary the Steelpoort River (Tubatse). It is bordered on the east by the Drakensberg Range and crossed by the Thaba Ya Sekhukhune in the south-east and the Leolo Mountains in the north.

Few historical locations remain and a guide is essential for this remote area.

Chapter 22

Death of King Cetshwayo and the Division of Zululand

King Cetshwayo had abandoned oNdini, and, accompanied only by his personal attendants, had listened to the sound of battle from behind a nearby hill. When the first fleeing warriors passed him, he rose quietly up and walked away. He made for the homestead of Mnyamana Buthelezi, and from there attempted to open negotiations with the British. They were prepared to offer him no terms, however, and he moved further north, into the remote Ngome forest. The British had despatched several patrols to capture him. With the king still at large, Wolseley gave orders for the searching troops to burn Zulu homesteads and carry off cattle in any area where the king was suspected to be hiding. Parties of mounted troops had been sent into the furthest corners of Zululand to find the king, with authority to freely engage in brutality to gain information. In one savage act, soldiers interrogated Chief Mpopha of the Hlabisa clan. He was first beaten and then questioned by soldiers using heated bayonet tips, a tactic that quickly paid off. It was not long before troops, led by Major Marter, discovered the king's former friend, Mnyamana, who avoided the bayonet treatment by warning the British that the king was hiding at a location in the Ngome Forest.

On 28 August the king was tracked down to a remote village by Marter. There was little the king could do, and after a short conversation, he quietly gave himself up. Marter treated his prisoner with dignity, though two of the king's servants were shot when they tried to run off. A tent was provided for him and his wives, and the 60th Rifles mounted a guard over it. For two days, he remained in camp while transport was arranged. Colonel Clarke gave responsibility for interpreting between himself and the royal party to Captain Harford, a fluent Zulu speaker.

The king was taken to the camp of Chelmsford's successor, Wolseley, near the burned-out ruins of his oNdini homestead, where he was officially told that he was to be exiled from Zululand. He was then escorted to Port Durnford on

THE DEATH OF KING CETSHWAYO
8 February 1884
AND THE DIVISION OF ZULULAND

1. Feb 1883 following his exile King Cetshwayo was brought back to Zululand and re-installed at Ulundi.

Not to scale

7. King Cetshwayo buried near the remote Mome Gorge.

2. On the king's return to Ulundi his supporters had already quarrelled with Chief Zibhebhu who had begun plotting against the king. A protracted and vicious civil war then broke out.

Attack route of Mandhlakazi.

NATAL   Eshowe.

3. In July 1883 Chief Zibhebhu began raiding into the king's domain so the king's followers sent 5,000 warriors from the Usuthu to drive Zibhebhu back. But it was a trap which enabled Zibhebhu to launch a surprise attack on Cetshwayo's rebuilt Ulundi *amakanda*. The royalists were heavily defeated and over 60 of the most important chiefs loyal to the king were killed. These included Ntshingwayo, who had commanded at Isandlwana and Khambula, and Sihayo, whose sons' actions had precipitated the British ultimatum which started the 1879 war.

4. The Mandhlakazi warriors of Zibhebhu ransacked Ulundi.

ULUNDI

5. King Cetshwayo was wounded in the fighting and, on 17 Oct. 1883, and now a broken soul, he took refuge with the British Resident at Eshowe.

6. 8 Feb. 1884 King Cetshwayo died, believed by poisoning, perhaps by his own people.

White Umfolozi River

8. King Cetshwayo's son, Prince Dinuzulu, desperately attempted to salvage the royalist cause. Sporadic violence continued for four more years, during which Dinuzulu secured Boer help to defeat Zibhebhu, but which cost the lives of a number of the prominent supporters of the old order. In 1884 the Boers murdered Prince Dabulamanzi, who had commanded at Rorke's Drift. Dinuzulu, continually harassed by the colonial authorities, was eventually goaded into leading armed resistance against the British. In 1888 he was defeated and sent into exile on St Helena where he remained until 1898. He was returned to Zululand but only as a 'regional advisor'. For supporting the Bambatha uprising in 1908 he was sentenced to four years' in Pietermaritzburg Prison but was released when Louis Botha became Prime Minister. Supplied with free alcohol by the British, he died in 1913.

the coast and taken aboard the steamer *Natal*. Here he posed for some rather pained photographs – only the second ever photo-session he had agreed to. Accompanied by his *induna*, EmaKhosini kaZangqana, and some attendants and *isigodlo* girls, he was taken to Cape Town and lodged in apartments in the old Cape Castle. His kingdom had already been divided up among British appointees.

Once the initial shock of defeat and exile wore off, King Cetshwayo found himself not without influence on Zulu affairs. His celebrity was such that he received a string of visitors to his apartments, mostly passing British gentry, many of whom became sympathetic to his plight and were in a position to influence official attitudes. With the stability of Zululand collapsing, King Cetshwayo began increasingly to lobby to be allowed to return to his country, under British authority, to restore order. His personal circumstances improved when he was moved from the castle to a farm, Oude Moulen, on the Cape flats. Finally, in August 1882, he was granted permission to visit London to argue his case. He arrived, smartly dressed in European clothes, to find that he was something of a celebrity, and crowds gathered curious to see the victor of Isandlwana. On finding that his manner was dignified and regal, and not at all the scowling savage represented in the illustrated press, the London crowds cheered him through the streets. He was granted an audience with Queen Victoria at Osborne House on the Isle of Wight, and, while the Queen herself was wary of the man who had damaged Lord Chelmsford's reputation and destroyed the 1/24th, she presented him with a large silver mug as a souvenir and ordered her court artist to paint his portrait.

Diplomatically, the mission was only a partial success. The Colonial Office agreed that the king might be restored to Zululand, but only to part of his old kingdom. Large tracts of the country were to be set aside for those Zulus who had ruled in his absence – and who could not be expected to welcome his return – and he would not be allowed to re-establish the *amabutho* system. Nor was his return announced to his countrymen; he arrived back on Zulu soil on 10 January 1883 to find only a few Zulus waiting to greet him. He was escorted to his old capital by Sir Theophilus Shepstone – who had 'crowned' him a decade before, and who had come out of retirement for the occasion. Once news of his return spread, his old supporters, *amakhosi*, *izinduna* and commoners alike flocked to renew their allegiance.

King Cetshwayo began rebuilding a new version of oNdini, not far from the complex destroyed in 1879. It was a smaller affair – perhaps just 1,000 huts – but still an impressive statement of his authority. He was, however, supervised by a British Resident, and he found the country deeply divided by several years of friction between his supporters and the appointees set up by the British. In particular, his followers bitterly resented the oppression they had suffered at the hands of his erstwhile general, *inkosi* Zibhebhu kaMapitha, and they were keen to be revenged upon him. Probably without King Cetshwayo's knowledge – and certainly without his sanction – a number of royalist supporters assembled an army in March to attack Zibhebhu. Zibhebhu was equal to the challenge and on the 30th he routed the royalists in the Msebe valley and destroyed them utterly. Civil war then broke out.

The attack caused consternation at oNdini. Cetshwayo assembled many of his most prominent advisors to discuss the crisis, and, despite the British ban on the *amabutho*, summoned those who still recognized their old allegiances. Before he could react, however, Zibhebhu struck first. At dawn on 21 July 1883, one of the women serving at oNdini was gathering water from a stream when she noticed a line of warriors silhouetted against the dim sky, advancing rapidly. Zibhebhu had made a daring night march with 3,000 warriors and was advancing to attack oNdini itself. As soon as word spread, the royalist warriors hurried out of their huts, but their commanders were still in agitated discussion with the king when Zibhebhu fell upon them. Urged to flee, Cetshwayo replied, 'Am I to run away from my dog?' Yet, the royalist stand soon collapsed in confusion, and flight was the only option. Most of the young warriors were fit enough to run away, but many of the king's elderly councillors were overtaken and killed. King Cetshwayo was led away on horseback, but not far from oNdini, the horse stumbled. Taking refuge in a small thicket, he was spotted by two young warriors from Zibhebhu's army, who hurled spears at him, striking him in the thigh. Even under such circumstances he maintained his composure. 'Do you stab me, Halijana son of Sumfula?' he asked, recognizing one of his assailants. 'I am your king!' Awestruck, the young warriors assisted him in dressing the wounds and helped him on his way.

Cetshwayo escaped the slaughter and made his way to the territory of inkosi Sigananda kaSokufa, head of the Cube people, a staunch loyalist who lived in the rugged country above the Thukela River. Here he hid for a while in a cave at the head of the Mome stream until, in October, he surrendered himself to the British authorities in Eshowe. He was allowed to live in a small homestead away from the British Residency. From here, for a second time, he attempted to rebuild his fortunes and he was visited by a trickle of leading royalists. In fact, his defeat had been comprehensive, and local British officials, who had been wary in any case of his restoration, refused to assist him. Then, suddenly, on the morning of 8 February 1884, Cetshwayo kaMpande collapsed and died. A British doctor examined the body but was refused permission to conduct an autopsy; he officially gave the cause of death as heart failure, but privately suggested Cetshwayo may have been poisoned. Two months later, Dinuzulu was proclaimed king.

Cetshwayo's supporters were determined to lay his body to rest away from the malicious influence of both the British and anti-royalists. After the necessary rites – the body was wrapped in a fresh bull's hide and smothered in blankets and allowed to desiccate in the heat of a closed hut – his remains were taken by wagon back to inkosi Sigananda's territory and buried not far from the Mome Gorge. The wagon was left on the spot and allowed to decay; its remains can now be seen in the Zulu Cultural Museum at oNdini.

Ironically, after his death – which had resulted from powerful divisions within the country, unleashed by the British invasion – King Cetshwayo's image came

The author and David Rattray at King Cetshwayo's grave.

Author and David Rattray on the 'track only' route to King Cetshwayo's grave.

increasingly to be seen as a unifying one. He was seen by Africans suffering under the reality of colonial rule as the representative of a golden age of power and independence. In 1906, when African discontent broke into violence over the issue of a newly implemented poll tax, the 'rebels' sought to draw on the mystique of King Cetshwayo's name to unify their movement. The king's grave was used as a rallying point for the rebellion, and, in a final bitter irony, it was nearby, in the Mome Gorge, that colonial forces inflicted a crushing defeat on one of the last traditionalist armies raised in Zululand.

The traditions of the Zulu *amabutho* continued to shape the defiant attitudes of the Zulus towards colonial authority well into the twentieth century. In 1906, Africans living in Natal finally took up arms to protest the harsh levels of taxation imposed upon them. One of the few Zulu chiefs to openly support them was Mehlokazulu kaSihayo. Mehlokazulu had served throughout the Anglo-Zulu War as an officer in the iNgobamakhosi Regiment, and, in 1906, he threw in his lot with the rebel leader, Bambatha. But the balance of power had swung even more in favour of the Europeans, and the rebel army was crushed at the Battle of Mome Gorge, where both Bambatha and Mehlokazulu were killed.

Chapter 23

The Boer Attack on the British at Bronkhorstspruit, December 1880

In 1879 Britain had gone to war against the Zulus partially to facilitate Boer farming expansion into Zululand. Yet, with minor exceptions, the Boers refused to participate in any action against the Zulus. By the following year, ever increasing numbers of Boers were smarting from the 1877 annexation of their Transvaal, which was slowly fanning their collective rebellion. By the end of 1880, and buoyed up by unimpressive British tactics during the Anglo-Zulu War, the Boers believed they were strong enough to make a successful stand against annexation and secretly renounced British rule.

A year later, on 5 December 1880, two companies of the 94th Regiment under the command of Colonel Anstruther, together with medical, commissariat staff and some families – 262 souls in all – set off from their base at Lydenburg to march the 180 miles to reinforce Pretoria. On 13 December 4,000 Boer burghers secretly met near Pretoria under President Kruger and Piet Joubert to proclaim the restoration of the republic. They decided to take immediate military action and despatched three commandos, one to intercept the 94th Regiment marching from its base at Lydenburg to strengthen the British garrison at Pretoria. Another went to Potchefstroom, and the third marched off to the border to discourage any British attempt to send reinforcements from Natal.

Unaware of the Boer action, Anstruther had already delayed his column's advance from Lydenburg for a week while extra wagons were hired from local Boer farmers. Because there were no other available wagons, exorbitant rates were demanded, which Anstruther reckoned would cost £1,000 in total. Once the column had obtained the requisite wagons, the forty-wagon column set off. Their progress was limited to about 8 miles each day due to the condition of the track and numerous streams that had to be negotiated. On 17 December, Anstruther received a warning the Boers were becoming hostile and to exercise caution. He wrote that the Boer families along the route were 'friendly and

BOER ATTACK ON BRITISH COLUMN BRONKHORSTSPRUIT, 20 December 1880.

TRANSVAAL
(annexed by Britain in 1877)

8. On seeing their rider's white flag thrown down the Boers opened fire. Anstruther was shot and wounded six times, all officers and most NCOs were killed or wounded, as were more than half the soldiers.

9. Anstruther gave the order to surrender. Ignoring the wounded the Boers disarmed the soldiers then plundered the column.

7. Col. Anstruther refused the ultimatum and gave the order to close ranks.

6. The Boer commando of 800 riders under Comdt. Joubert approached the column to within 130 yards and took up firing positions behind boulders.

10. It was left to the survivors to tend the wounded and bury their dead, under a small Boer guard.

Track to Pretoria 40 miles.

11. Sgt. Maistre wrapped the Colours around his body and smuggled them out to safety. He was awarded the Distinguished Conduct Medal.

Lightly wooded with small thorn trees.

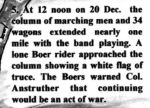

5. At 12 noon on 20 Dec. the column of marching men and 34 wagons extended nearly one mile with the band playing. A lone Boer rider approached the column showing a white flag of truce. The Boers warned Col. Anstruther that continuing would be an act of war.

12. Under a white flag of truce the Boers attacked a column that included women and children. Condemnation of the Boers' action followed.

4. The following morning they failed to see any significance in a large number of saddled Boer horses in a paddock.

13. The 94th lost one officer and 73 men killed in the attack.

3. 18 December. The column was wet and weary having had to struggle across the flooded Oliphants River.

14. Mrs Anne Fox, although wounded, tended the wounded. She was later awarded the Royal Red Cross along with Mrs Maistre and Mrs Smith. Mrs Fox later died of her injuries.

Oliphants River.

2. 17th Dec. A message was received by Col. Anstruther that the Boers were hostile and to exercise caution.

To Lydenburg 100 miles.

Not to scale.

1. On 5 December, two companies of the 94th Regiment under Colonel Anstruther, together with medical, commissariat staff and families, some 262 souls in all, departed Lydenburg to march to reinforce Pretoria. The Boers unexpectedly proclaimed the Transvaal a South African Republic on the 13th December. The column were unaware of the Boer self-proclaimed declaration of independence.

High ground overlooking track

Boer attack

Boulders.

Boulders.

Boulders.

civil', even if a regular comment was 'if you don't give us back the Transvaal, we'll fight like cats', which Anstruther took as friendly banter, observing, 'they have, I am sure, no intention of fighting, though if we are firm with them, as I hope we will be, there might be one or two little disturbances'.

By 19 December, the column was wet and weary, having had to cross the flooded Oliphants River. Early the following morning, they paused at a Boer farm to purchase fresh provisions and then make amends after some of the soldiers had stolen fruit from the farmer's orchard. Little was made of the incident, and the stolen fruit was paid for with an apology. At the time, Anstruther noticed an unaccountable number of horses corralled around the farm, all saddled and ready to depart, but failed to notice their significance. Unbeknown to Anstruther, the farm was the rendezvous for the Boers detailed to intercept the column, but, taken by surprise by the arriving British, the Boers had hidden themselves in some outbuildings and had no option but to leave their horses in full view of the approaching British column.

At about 10.00 am, the column ignored the tethered Boer horses and continued on its way with the intention of stopping for the night at a crossing point at the Bronkhorst stream just a few miles distant. The whole column of marching men and thirty-four wagons extended nearly a mile and, blissfully, continued on its way with the band playing. It was about 2 miles from the intended camp site when a Boer rider approached the leading wagons showing a white flag of truce. The British were unsure what was happening, but Anstruther had the presence of mind to give the order to close ranks. The order was passed down the column, and the band stopped playing. The rider presented Anstruther with an ultimatum, counter-signed by Paul Kruger. The order instructed Anstruther not to continue beyond the Bronkhorst stream until diplomatic negotiations between the British and Boers were resolved. It warned that the troops' advance beyond the stream would be construed by the Boers as an act of war. The rider added that two minutes would be allowed for the column commander to decide his course of action. The main Boer commando, some 200 riders, under the protection of the white flag, then approached the column to within 150 yards and positioned themselves behind rocks and trees. According to witnesses, Anstruther replied:

I have orders to proceed with all possible dispatch to Pretoria and to Pretoria I am going, but tell the Commandant I have no wish to meet him in hostile spirit.

While showing a white flag of truce, the Boers had intended attacking a column that included women and children. Widespread condemnation of the Boers' action followed. The rider with the white flag then threw it down, a signal to the Boers to open fire on the helpless and unsuspecting column. The unprotected wagons and soldiers, many of whom were unarmed, were sitting targets for the Boer marksmen, and within minutes, Anstruther was shot and wounded six times, and all the officers and most of the NCOs were wounded, as were more than half the soldiers.

To save the lives of the remainder, the seriously wounded Anstruther gave the order to cease firing and to hoist something white to signify their surrender. This done, firing ceased on both sides, and the Boers closed in. The Boers then collected up all available weapons and drove off the wagons containing arms and ammunition and anything else they considered of use or value. The column conductor, Mr Egerton, received permission to ride to Pretoria to get medical assistance. Colour Sergeant Maistre wrapped the Colours around his body and smuggled them out to safety. For his actions in saving the Colours, Maistre was awarded the Distinguished Conduct Medal. Under a Boer guard, the column survivors were left to fend for themselves as best they could, tending the wounded and burying their dead. The following day, the fit survivors were marched off by the Boers to Heidelberg and the less serious casualties escorted to Pretoria. A makeshift British hospital was constructed at Bronkhorstspruit for the seriously wounded, and there it remained for three further months before their travel to Pretoria was permitted.

The Boer attack on the unsuspecting column was premeditated and shocking in its sudden and wilful execution. Their objective was to cause the most serious damage as swiftly as possible in order to send a shock message to the procrastinating British to resolve Boer claims for independence. The 94th suffered 58 per cent casualties; they lost one officer, Lieutenant Harrison, and seventy-three men killed in the carnage of the attack. Another four officers and ninety men received wounds, of which three officers, Anstruther (who lost a leg), Captain Nairne and Captain MacSwiney, and eighteen men, later died. One officer and 105 men became prisoners of the Boers. The Boers lost one killed and four wounded.

At the conclusion of the war, the 94th Regiment remained in the Transvaal until the final ratification of the peace convention with the Boers was signed, and then, on 5 November 1881, they commenced their march back to Natal.

On 24 March 1882, seven companies embarked on the *Dublin Castle* and sailed for Queenstown, Cork in Ireland where they arrived on 20 April.

At home, there were celebrations and campaign medals for the survivors. There had been considerable anger in the British press at the Boers' disregard of their own flag of truce, but by the time the regiment returned home, the first Boer conflict was over and Bronkhorstspruit was rarely mentioned.

Location

Bronkhorstspruit is a town 50km east of Pretoria, Gauteng, South Africa along the N4 highway towards Witbank. Today there is a memorial next to the road, and the graves are well tended. Local residents would be able to indicate this location.

Bronkhorstspruit memorial today.

Appendix I

Decorations and Medals of the Anglo-Zulu War of 1879

Anglo-Zulu War decorations and medals awarded

ISANDLWANA, 22 January 1879
(Sotondosa's Drift, near Rorke's Drift)
VICTORIA CROSS
Private S. Wassall, 80th Regt.
Lieutenant N.J.A. Coghill 1/24th Regt. Posthumously awarded in 1907.
Lieutenant T. Melvill 1/24th Regt. Posthumously awarded in 1907.

RORKE'S DRIFT, 22 and 23 January 1879
VICTORIA CROSS
Lieutenant J.R.M. Chard RE
Lieutenant G. Bromhead 2/24th Regt.
Surgeon J.H. Reynolds, Army Medical Department
Acting Assistant Commissary J.L. Dalton, Commissary Department
Corporal F.C. Schiess, Natal Native Contingent
Corporal W.W. Allen 2/24th Regt.
Private F. Hitch 2/24th Regt.
Private A.H. Hook 2/24th Regt
Private J. Williams 2/24th Regt.
Private R. Jones 2/24th Regt.
Private W. Jones 2/24th Regt.

DISTINGUISHED CONDUCT MEDAL
Colour Sergeant F. Bourne, 2/24th Regt.
Corporal M. McMahon, Army Medical Corps (withdrawn for theft and desertion).
Second Corporal F. Attwood, Army Service Corps.
Wheeler J. Cantwell, Royal Artillery
Private W. Roy 1/24th Regt.

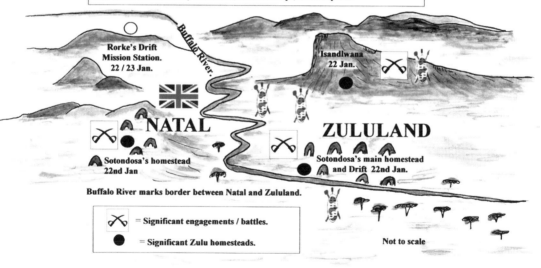

DECORATIONS AND MEDALS
of the Anglo-Zulu War of 1879

↑
N

Ntombe River.
12 March

Khambula.
29 March

Hlobane Mountain.
28 March

White Mfolozi
River 3 July

Ulundi.
4 July

No decorations were issued for the actions at Gingindlovu or Nyezane. Whilst not a decoration, Sgt. C. Jenkins of the Cape Mounted Rifles was personally thanked by Chelmsford for his bravery in leading a charge against the Zulus at Nyezane. He was given an immediate field promotion to Lieutenant, a rare reward especially as it included an enhanced pension.

The Royal Red Cross   (known as the nurses' Victoria Cross).
Post war, and on learning of the bravery of the twelve nurses who participated in the Anglo-Zulu War, Queen Victoria instigated the RRC for civilian nurses who took part in the campaign but who were ineligible to receive military decorations. An example is Sister Janet Wells who, in her early twenties, served on the British front line at Utrecht and finished her field service in South Africa at Rorke's Drift. While at the Cape *en route* to London she was requested to treat an unwell King Cetshwayo.
Royal Red Crosses were presented to the six civilian Stafford House Nurses and the six Army Hospital Corps nurses for their service in the war.
The citation is for...
'The zeal and devotion in providing for and nursing sick and wounded sailors, soldiers and others with the Army in the field, on board ships, or in hospitals.'

Rorke's Drift
Mission Station.
22 / 23 Jan.

Buffalo River.

Isandlwana
22 Jan.

NATAL

ZULULAND

Sotondosa's homestead
22nd Jan

Sotondosa's main homestead
and Drift 22nd Jan.

Buffalo River marks border between Natal and Zululand.

⚔ = Significant engagements / battles.

● = Significant Zulu homesteads.

Not to scale

NTOMBE RIVER, 12 March 1879
VICTORIA CROSS
Sergeant A.C. Booth, 80th Regt.

HLOBANE MOUNTAIN, 28 March 1879
VICTORIA CROSS
Brevet Lieutenant Colonel R.H. Buller, 60th Rifles
Major W.K. Leet, 1/13th Regt.[6]
Lieutenant H. Lysons, 90th Regt.
Lieutenant E.S. Browne, 1/24th Regt.
Private E. Fowler, 90th Regt.

DISTINGUISHED CONDUCT MEDAL
Corporal W.D. Vinnicombe, Frontier Light Horse
Trooper R. Brown, Frontier Light Horse
Private J. Power, 1/24th Regt.
Bugler A. Walkinshaw, 90th Light Infantry

KHAMBULA, 29 March 1879
DISTINGUISHED CONDUCT MEDAL
Troop Sergeant Major Learda, Natal Native Horse
Acting Sergeant E. Quigley, 1/13th Regt.
Private A. Page, 1/13th Regt.

WHITE MFOLOZI RIVER, 3 July 1879
VICTORIA CROSS
Captain Lord W.L. de la P. Beresford, 9th Lancers
Sergeant C.D. D'Arcy, Frontier Light Horse
Sergeant E. O'Toole, Frontier Light Horse

DISTINGUISHED CONDUCT MEDAL
Troop Sergeant Major S. Kambula, Natal Native Horse

---

6. Major Leet applied directly to a friend in the War Office for the VC, and he uniquely received it. He is variously referred to as Leet or Knox-Leet.

ULUNDI, 4 July 1879
DISTINGUISHED CONDUCT MEDAL
Colour Sergeant J. Phillips, 58th Regt.
Gunner W. Moorhead, Royal Artillery

Victoria Crosses <u>not</u> awarded

Lieutenant Harford at Sihayo's Homestead. Following the engagement, Chelmsford called for Lieutenant Harford and suggested he should receive a decoration for his bravery. Embarrassed in front of senior officers, Harford politely declined out of courtesy to Chelmsford. The matter was never raised again, and Harford regretted his moment of politeness for the remainder of his long service.

Trooper Barker, Natal Carbineers. Recommended by Brigadier Wood for surrendering his horse to his adjutant, Lieutenant Higginson, after Isandlwana. Wood's recommendation was rejected by the War Office in London on the grounds that too many Victoria Crosses had already been issued.

Captain Duck, Veterinary Department. Nominated by Buller for bravery at Hlobane. The application was rejected on the grounds he had no right to be there.

No decorations were issued for the actions at Gingindlovu or Nyezane. Whilst not a decoration, Sergeant C. Jenkins of the Cape Mounted Rifles, was personally thanked by Chelmsford for his bravery in leading a charge against the Zulus at Nyezane. He was given an immediate field promotion to lieutenant, a rare reward, as it included an enhanced pension.

The Royal Red Cross. Six Crosses each were presented to the nurses of the Stafford House and the Army Hospital Corps. Known as The Nurses' VC, it was first issued to nurses who took part in the South Africa campaign. The decoration was instigated at the request of Queen Victoria as a result her hearing of the bravery of the twelve nurses who took part in the Anglo-Zulu War. The citation is for:

> The zeal and devotion in providing for and nursing sick and wounded sailors, soldiers and others with the Army in the field, on board ships, or in hospitals.

Appendix II

Sister Janet: The Rorke's Drift Nurse

In 2003 the author had his attention drawn to a suitcase, found in an attic in Sussex, that contained scrapbooks, drawings, sketches, letters and medals of a young nurse, Sister Janet Wells, who had served at Utrecht in the Anglo-Zulu War and who was subsequently decorated by Queen Victoria. This was an astonishing find that became the subject of books, articles and a BBC television programme. A recently discovered letter, from David Rattray of Fugitives' Drift Lodge, explains:

Florence Nightingale was the first recipient of the Royal Red Cross, with Sister Janet Wells not far behind. She was only 18 years old when she was posted to Zululand to command a medical post. She earned the nickname 'Angel of Mercy'.

She performed numerous operations, tended the sick and wounded and brought an air of discipline, tempered by her charm and femininity, into a chaotic and desperate situation. Towards the end of the war, she was sent to Rorke's Drift, where she administered to the remaining garrison. She walked the battlefields of Rorke's Drift and Isandlwana, where she collected flowers for her scrapbooks – already containing many sketches and photographs, which survive to this day.

After the war, she returned to her home and family in London, just in time for her twentieth birthday. Recognition by Queen Victoria followed, who decorated her with the Royal Red Cross, the nursing equivalent of the Victoria Cross. She was the second recipient of the award; the previous recipient was Florence Nightingale.

Hers is an amazing account, of bravery and determination, which I commend to everyone who loves adventure; it will especially fascinate students of the Anglo-Zulu War, to whom this account will come, I am sure, as something of a surprise.

David Rattray

Appendix III

Gold Fever at Rorke's Drift

After peace broke out following the 1879 war, thankfully for the isolated Rorke's Drift community, the area was too far from the basic road network and of no use to any commercial enterprise. Even during the following Boer Wars, the nearest combatants came to Rorke's Drift was some 30 miles away at Dundee, with a small outpost at Helpmakaar. But with South Africa becoming famous for its mineral wealth in the 1880s, it was not too long before gold fever spread from the Transvaal to the steep and rocky Buffalo River gorges near Rorke's and Fugitives' drifts.

The search for gold had originally started a mile south of the drifts, and in one lucky period, some 800 ounces of gold were recovered, and then the seam ran out. The prospectors left, but one keen ex-sailor from HMS *Boadicea*, known as Barclay, stayed on, convinced he would make his fortune. He purchased several mining options in the area including Fugitives' Drift, where he prospected for several months. From the pump house at the drift, which today supplies water to the nearby Fugitives' Drift Lodge, the original workings built by Barclay can still be seen, as can the mineshaft built into the base of the cliff overlooking the river, known to the local Zulus as 'Albert's Shaft'. Local folklore suggests Barclay never found any gold, and worse, it is not known what happened to him.

Diamond fever had a similar affect when it reached the Rorke's Drift area but only as a result of a simple human error. In 1920, Mr Ekron, the farmer who owned Petroscar Farm near the fugitives' graves, found two rough diamonds in a small pool next to the river. He took them for verification to a Mr Meyer at Dundee who, without telling Ekron, swiftly purchased the land surrounding the pool. Local folklore remembers Meyer paying twelve times the current value for the land.

Stone sifting equipment was transported to the site and washing began. For months work progressed but nothing was found. Ekron occasionally passed by and one day came across Meyer watching the sluicing operation. Ekron, by accident or design, mentioned that this was the very place where his ostriches once gathered to drink. Meyer knew Ekron had once owned a flock that had been reared for their feathers, but the venture failed, and he asked Ekron where the ostriches had come from, to which Ekron replied 'from the diamond fields at Kimberley where they had been used as "guard dogs" to prevent thieves scavenging loose diamonds'. On realizing the diamonds found by Ekron had been passed by one of the Kimberley ostriches, the Meyer diamond venture closed down.

Apart from the steady gentle stream of battlefield visitors to Rorke's Drift, little else has happened except we have lost three lodge owner friends at Rorke's Drift; namely, the recent murders of David Rattray at Fugitives' Drift Lodge and Rob Gerrard at Isandlwana Lodge, followed by the death of Charles Aitkenhead when his new Rorke's Drift Lodge caught fire.

Appendix IV

The Defences at Rorke's Drift

Until recently the general belief, featured in the film *Zulu*, held that the mission station was defended with mealie sacks only as the Zulus approached for their attack. However, two contemporary and independent written accounts in letters home, from people present, confirm the two buildings were fortified from 11 January, the work supervised by Assistant Commissary Dalton. These important letters were written by Lieutenant Harford, on loan to the NNC from the 99th Regiment, and by August Hammar, Reverend Witt's friend, left by Witt to protect his interests at the Drift. Both were present throughout the preparation of the defences.

Curiously, Witt could not speak English and most British accounts of those present, and of most historians, naturally presumed August Hammar was Witt. But Witt had departed the Drift before the British arrived in order to join his family fleeing to Durban.

Appendix V

Laying the Blame

Chelmsford's Original Battle Orders

These orders, kept in a basement tin box at the Royal Engineers Museum, Gillingham, were first seen by the author in 2000. They solved the mystery of why Colonel Pulleine deployed his men so far from the camp. Until their discovery, there had been no mention of the orders, and, unsurprisingly, Lord Chelmsford never declared their existence as they would have vindicated Colonel Pulleine of the blame of having his men so far from the camp, thus allowing the Zulus to out-flank and surround the position.

At the time, Chelmsford's staff officer, Colonel Crealock, had falsely claimed to have ordered Durnford to Isandlwana to 'Take command of the camp'. If correct, as the new camp commander, Durnford would have inherited these non-existent orders to defend the camp. When at 11.45 am Durnford left Isandlwana in charge of Colonel Pulleine, Chelmsford claimed Durnford was disobeying these orders and weakened the garrison. Had his orders been followed, claimed Chelmsford falsely, there would have been no disaster. Chelmsford later damningly stated in his Isandlwana speech in Parliament:

> In the final analysis it was Durnford's disregard of orders that brought about its destruction.

And that was the end of the matter, until a Trooper Pearse, who was searching the battlefield for his lost brother, also a trooper, discovered Durnford's body. He removed two documents from the body. The first was Lord Chelmsford's order dated 19 January. This order makes it clear that Durnford's column was to co-operate with No.3 column, *not* as part of it. In the absence of any specific order from Chelmsford on the morning of 22 January, there was no reason for Durnford to think he was supposed to take command from Colonel Pulleine at Isandlwana. Chelmsford must have presumed there was no trace of the incriminating order later recovered by Pearse. For Chelmsford, Durnford was the perfect scapegoat for the British defeat at Isandlwana – he was dead. The second document recovered from Durnford's body was Durnford's copy of Chelmsford's 'Orders to Column Commanders' and dealt with troop positions when under attack, which Pulleine had obeyed when faced with the rapidly approaching Zulu army; but it was too late to react, the troops at Isandlwana were too thinly deployed and too far from the camp.

Pulleine's total misunderstanding of Zulu tactics ensured their victory, as did his deployment of his troops so far away from his camp headquarters. Indeed, they were so far out that neither they, nor the attacking Zulus, could be seen by Pulleine and his headquarters staff. The reason, as seen from the missing orders, was because he was obeying to the letter the orders he had received from Chelmsford, orders given to all five column commanders, orders that detailed the tactics to be used in the event of a Zulu attack. If further evidence is required, then it should be pointed out that identical tactics had coincidentally been used that very same morning at two separate locations, both just 50 miles from Isandlwana; at Nyzane, Colonel Pearson's Coastal Column came under a sustained Zulu attack, and at Hlobane by Colonel Wood when

Pages four and five of Chelmsford's original orders to Durnford.

attacking Zulu positions. Pulleine had faithfully deployed his force according to Chelmsford's orders. Such tactics were doomed to fail in a defensive position. They were never used again against the Zulus

Perhaps this is another reason why these orders were never referred to by Chelmsford's staff officers at the subsequent court of inquiry, or thereafter. Their publication would have completely vindicated Pulleine and incriminated Chelmsford. Pulleine's deployment of his experienced troops in an extended line so far out from the Isandlwana camp was contemptuously considered by many contemporary writers and has mystified most military

Chelmford's orders to Durnford.

historians. Pulleine had no battle experience and had little warning of the impending disaster – yet the deployment was clearly not his own idea. No historian has ever produced evidence that the experienced 1/24th officers ever openly challenged the extended deployment so far from the camp, although Captain Stafford of the NNC recalled in his memoirs that when Durnford arrived at Pulleine's tent, Durnford expressed considerable alarm at the distant disposition of British troops.

As the senior officer at Isandlwana, it was logical that Pulleine would follow Chelmsford's orders and so he deployed his officers and men according to the plan drawn in these orders. No wonder that the officers of the 24th thus deployed did not openly demur. For an examination of these orders, see my *Isandlwana – How the Zulus Humbled the British Empire'* published by Pen & Sword.

Appendix VI

Medal Confusion: Who was Awarded the South Africa Campaign Medal?

My battlefield guests were invariably Anglo-Zulu War enthusiasts and a number were also medal collectors, owning or seeking to own a 24th Regiment South Africa campaign medal, especially if the participant had been at Isandlwana, Rorke's Drift or seen action. Such medals have long been among the most prized by medal collectors, which is reflected by their high and ever rising prices. But I always emphasise caution, as many such South Africa campaign medals awarded to the 24th Regiment were also awarded to the replacements, from other units of the regiment who were lost at Isandlwana and Rorke's Drift.

As soon as tidings of the disaster at Isandlwana reached England, volunteers were called for to re-form the 1st Battalion, 24th Regiment, and a draft of 520 non-commissioned officers and men was soon furnished by the following regiments:

> 1st battalion 8th, 1st battalion 11th, 1st battalion 18th, 2nd battalion 18th, 1st battalion 23rd, 2nd battalion 25th, 32nd, 37th, 38th, 45th, 50th, 55th, 60th, 86th, 87th, 103rd, 108th, and 109th.

They collected at Aldershot, under the command of Lieutenant Colonel H.F. Davies of the Grenadier Guards, most of the men were raw recruits and many had never fired a Martini-Henry rifle. The draft embarked at Woolwich, in the *Clyde*, on 1 March 1879. These temporary replacements for the new 1st Battalion, 24th Regiment would also receive the same campaign medal as the recipients present at Isandlwana and Rorke's Drift, although most were posted back to their original units after the war. So, they received the South Africa Medal for temporarily serving with the regiment, even though the 24th Regiment was not their parent unit. Although some of these temporary replacements did take part in the later Battle of Ulundi, others never entered

Zululand: their medals have no medal clasp, which indicates that the recipients remained in Natal without crossing into Zululand.

Rorke's Drift defenders were a curious exception as they were all given the clasp to their medal, yet many didn't cross into Zululand. It raises another interesting question: as the 2nd Battalion did not arrive in South Africa until 1878, why did they have 1877–8–9 on their medal bar? So the answer to the original question remains complex, necessitating caution. Regimental nominal rolls should always be consulted to establish where a medal recipient served.

Appendix VII

The Welsh Question

When lecturing at Rorke's Drift and Isandlwana, guests frequently asked about the name and composition of the 24th Regiment at the time of Rorke's Drift and Isandlwana, questions that arose from the powerful but misleading Welsh influence portrayed in the film '*Zulu*'. Guests knew I had served as an officer in The Welch Regiment and that I was an Englishman. For me, the question was not an issue, simply because, at the time of the Anglo-Zulu War in 1879, the 24th Regiment was the 2nd Warwickshire Regiment, with its recruits coming mainly from the Birmingham and Tamworth areas. Although the regimental depot had been in Brecon since 1873, its location was by chance rather than design, and it stayed that way until 1881 when the regiment became The South Wales Borderers.

Before the Anglo-Zulu War, the 24th had no special depot for recruiting; had it tried recruiting in Wales, or specifically Brecon, it would have encountered a logistical problem as Wales was sparsely populated until the expansion of the coal, iron and steel industries in the late nineteenth century. For example, until 1880, Brecon had a static population of only 5,000 people covering a wide rural area with only 2,551 males of all ages, so the number of fit men of recruiting age was, therefore, very small.

The 1st Battalion had seen continuous service in various Mediterranean garrisons for the eight years prior to arriving in South Africa on 4 February 1875. At this point in time, the 1st Battalion's link with Wales was, at the very best, tenuous; indeed, its regimental march was *The Warwickshire Lads* composed for the Shakespearean Centenary Celebrations at Stratford-on-Avon in 1769.

Private Robert Jones VC, 2/24th born at Monmouthshire (then an English county), was awarded the Victoria Cross for his part in the defence of Rorke's Drift. To ponder whether he was English or Welsh probably never occurred to him when writing about his experiences:

On the 22nd January 1879, the Zulus attacked us, we being only a small band of English soldiers. My thought was only to fight as an English soldier ought to for his most gracious Sovereign, Queen Victoria, and for the benefit of old England.

In view of the 1881 change in designation of the 24th into the South Wales Borderers, and the emphasis on Welsh characters in 'Zulu', battlefield visitors were invariably curious as to the actual representation of Welshmen who had served in the two battalions at Isandlwana and Rorke's Drift. With regard to the 1/24th lost at Isandlwana, there was virtually no connection with Wales, as the battalion had neither served in the UK since 1867 nor ever recruited from Wales. Indeed, when the news of the loss of the 1/24th reached Britain, *The Daily News* commented; 'Death had prematurely visited hundreds of peaceful and happy homes in England', which sadly ignored the high proportion of Irishmen serving in both battalions.

The 2/24th certainly had a small proportion of Welshmen serving in its ranks (born, or living in Wales when recruited).

The actual origin of soldiers of the 24th Regiment who defended Rorke's Drift is as follows:

1st Battalion, 24th Regiment
4 soldiers from:

   1 Staffordshire, England
   1 Midlothian, Scotland
   1 Dublin, Ireland
   1 Peshawar, India (of British parents)

2nd Battalion, 24th Regiment
47 English soldiers from:

   1 each from; Cheshire; Gloucestershire; Leicestershire; Nottinghamshire; Surrey; Sussex; Worcestershire; Yorkshire
   2 each from; Kent and Middlesex
   3 each from Herefordshire and Warwickshire
   4 from Somerset

9 from Lancashire

11 from London

5 from Monmouthshire (it was an English county in 1879 and became Welsh in 1976 following the boundary re-organization)

13 Irish soldiers from:

1 each from Antrim and Limerick

2 each from Clare, Cork, Kilkenny and Tipperary

3 from Dublin

5 Welsh soldiers from:

1 each from Breconshire and Pembrokeshire

3 from Glamorgan

Others

1 France

With regard to the 24th's Rorke's Drift VCs, Lieutenant Bromhead was born in France (to a Lincolnshire family); Hook was from Gloucestershire; Allen was from Northumbria born in Scotland; Hitch was a Londoner; William Jones was from Worcestershire; Robert Jones and John Fielding (alias Williams) were from Monmouthshire (then an English county); and Fielding was anyway Irish, although hailing from Abergavenny.

So we are left with an academic if meaningless question, and the reality of a fine regiment. The spirit of the 24th Regiment is strongly maintained today by The Royal Welsh. Regardless of names, origins or who fought where, the regiment is one of the outstanding regiments of the British Army and, since becoming The South Wales Borderers in 1881, one with a distinct Welsh flair. Its motto is proudly displayed on the Regimental Colour – *Gwell Angau na Chywilydd* – Death rather than Dishonour.

On St David's Day, 1 March 2006, The Royal Welch Fusiliers (23rd Foot) amalgamated with The Royal Regiment of Wales to form The Royal Welsh (lineage 23rd, 24th, 41st and 69th Foot).

Appendix VIII

Disembowelling and Disarticulation

Battlefield visitors were always curious about one particular Zulu custom, a custom that was feared, misunderstood, and which tended to give many a Boer trekker and British soldiers sleepless nights, the Zulu post-battle cleansing tradition of disembowelling the enemy, usually with a knife-like weapon – rarely the assegai. The custom of disembowelling a fallen enemy, *qaqa*, was standard practice and was directly related to the Zulu view of the afterlife and its relationship with the world of the living. Part of this ritual involved slitting open the stomach of the slain enemy. To the Zulus, it was essential that those slain in battle or clan disputes had to be ritually disembowelled to free any incarcerated spirit and to protect the victor from absorbing any bad spirits previously possessed by their victim.

Under the African sun, any corpse will quickly putrefy and the gases given off by the early stages of decay cause the stomach to swell. In Zulu belief, this was the soul of the dead warrior vainly trying to escape to the after-life. The victor was obliged to open the stomach of his victim to allow the spirit to escape, failing which, the victor would be haunted by the ghost of his victim, who would inflict unmentionable horrors upon him, including causing his own stomach to swell until, eventually, the victor would go mad. As a final cleansing rite, usually after local skirmishes, the victor then had to have intercourse with a woman, not his wife, before returning to his clan. This practice ensured that

Beards on campaign.

any remaining trace of evil spirits would be left with the woman, leaving the victor clean and whole to return home. It also ensured that post-battle, the *impi* would rapidly and enthusiastically disperse from the battlefield for the purpose of religious cleansing. Zulu warriors were only accorded any real status when they had 'washed' their spears in the blood of a defeated enemy.

Archibald Forbes' graphic account in *The Daily News*, 10 July 1879, of the state of the bodies at the time of the first burial expedition to Isandlwana in May 1879 is graphic:

> Every man had been disembowelled, some were scalped, and others subject to yet ghastlier mutilations.

At Isandlwana, these mutilations included the disarticulation by the Zulus of the dead soldiers' jawbones for trophies, complete with beards. Facial hair was relatively unknown to the warriors and the luxurious beards worn by the soldiers fascinated them. Despite the soldiers' deep-seated fears that these mutilations were carried out before death, and therefore amounted to torture, there is no evidence that this was in fact the case. Interestingly, post Isandlwana, the practice of shaving became widespread throughout the army. Soldiers were prepared for the necessity of dying for their country but were reluctant to be disarticulated after death on the battlefield.

Appendix IX

Corporal Christian Ferdinand Schiess VC

Rorke's Drift visitors were understandably fascinated by the many accounts of the night's fighting. One character in particular stood out for his acknowledged bravery, especially as he fought on crutches. The fact that he was a Swiss national and, post battle, was believed to have existed in illness and poverty, added to the intrigue. Little is known about Schiess, so, who was this brave and enigmatic character and what was he doing at Rorke's Drift?

It is a sad fact that some survivors of the defence of Rorke's Drift had their lives cut tragically short by illness, or the dire circumstances in which they found themselves in later years. No individual epitomises this more than Corporal Schiess of the Natal Native Contingent, who died on board the troopship HMS *Serapis* on 14 December 1884 while being repatriated to England. He was buried at sea off the west coast of Africa: he was only 28 years old. The captain's log reads:

Sunday, 14 December 1884
10.20 am Departed this life, Mr F.C. Scheiss, VC

5.10 pm Stopped. Committed to the Deep the remains of the late Mr F.C. Schiess, VC

5.15 pm Proceeded

Ship's Noon observed Position: Lat S.13.00: Long W.7.24

Schiess seems to have packed a lot into his short life. Born on 7 April 1856 at Burgdorf, among the mountains of Switzerland, he was raised for some years in an orphanage. He was only 14 or 15 years old when he joined the French army where he is believed to have taken part in the Franco-Prussian War of 1870–71.

From Europe, he travelled to South Africa, where he eventually joined the NNC and achieved the rank of corporal. His heroics at Rorke's Drift are well documented and were such that the 'British-only' rule for the award of the

Victoria Cross was waived for this Swiss national. Schiess was two months short of his twenty-forth birthday when he received his VC from Sir Garnet Wolseley on 3 February 1880 in Pietermaritzburg. Immensely proud, he carried his medal to his dying day and it was found in his pocket before his burial; it is now on display in the National Army Museum.

The years between 1880 and his death in December 1884 are something of a mystery. The conventional narrative suggests he worked in the Durban Telegraph Office for some time after leaving the NNC, but then struggled to find work and ended up destitute and ill on the streets of Cape Town.

In late 1884, public donations bought him an 'indulgence' ticket to England on board HMS *Serapis*, which had just docked from India: he sadly died a few days into the voyage. News of the death of a VC hero in such circumstances was not greeted kindly in some quarters. For example, the British periodical, *Truth*, offered this rebuke in its issue of 15 January, 1885:

> The case of Corporal Schiess, V.C., does not look particularly creditable to his country. To what regiment Schiess belonged I do not know, but he served through the Zulu campaign, and was awarded the Victoria Cross for distinguished gallantry at Rorke's Drift. After the war he lapsed into absolute poverty at Natal and was lately in such a condition that a subscription was got up to pay his rations home as an indulgence passenger on the *Serapis*. Want and exposure, however, had so told on him that he died on the voyage. I dare say Schiess himself may have been partly to blame, but we ought to be able to turn a man who could win the Victoria Cross at Rorke's Drift to better account than this.

This article is not notable for its accuracy and it does contain the rather cryptic comment about Schiess himself being 'partly to blame', but it does express a sentiment that was shared in some circles. However, two years beyond the exploits at Rorke's Drift there is still no sign of the destitution or 'absolute poverty' that the article referred to.

However, further examination of contemporary records and publications casts doubt on this simplified account of Schiess's final years, certainly in terms of the timing. A short piece in *The York House* papers of 8 December 1880 provided more detail. The article reads:

From Natal I hear that large numbers of citizens have been flocking to commandant Baker's standard, that gentleman having volunteered to raise a corps of mounted men for service against the Basutos... Among the non-commissioned officers is the familiar figure of Sergeant Scheiss [*sic*] V.C., who was decorated with the Cross for valour, in recognition of his distinguished gallantry in Zululand.

From this, we can see that Schiess had not given up on military service after leaving the NNC and he was obviously a known figure. Proof of his continued service with this mounted troop came from the unlikely source of a provincial Lincolnshire newspaper, The *Stamford Mercury*. On 15 April 1881, under the heading '*With Baker's Horse in Basutoland*', it published a letter sent to Mr William Barton, the publisher of the newspaper, from his son, who was serving with Baker's Horse 'which was destined for employment against the Basutos'. The young Mr Barton recounted the following anecdote in his letter home, dated 2 February 1881:

I have been out the last few days – one of a party repairing the telegraph wires cut by the enemy; not a nice job for five fellows alone and about ten miles from camp. But we had a good man in charge – corporal Schiess, V.C., one of the Rorke's Drift heroes. He is a nice fellow and we are the best of friends. He was born in the Alps, and is Swiss. This mountainous country suits him. When we were out the other day we went and looked for some sham chamois. We were unsuccessful, of course. I think if he had seen some of the enemy it would not have been a sham. He is a dead shot.

There was to be one more twist to the story of Corporal Schiess in the unexpected setting of a royal visit to India by the Duke and Duchess of Connaught at the end of 1883. The following so-called 'incident' was reported widely in the press as the duke was inspecting troops at Allahabad (now Prayagraj) on 1 December 1883. The same article was printed almost word for word in several publications, including *The Times of India*, dated 18 December 1883:

On arrival of the special train at Allahabad on the 1st December with their Royal Highnesses the Duke and Duchess of Connaught (after being presented to the notabilities of the station), the Duke proceeded to inspect the guard of honour composed of a very strong muster of the E.I.R. Volunteers. Glancing over the men his quick eye detected one little fellow, Volunteer F.C. Schiess, in the ranks, on whose breast hung the Victoria Cross. With that readiness and good feeling so general with the members of the Royal Family, he at once stepped up to him and, kindly with interest, enquired where and how he had earned the distinguished decoration. I leave it to be imagined with what pride the gallant little fellow answered, possibly 'Sir, at Rorke's Drift', such being actually the case. Unfortunately, poor Schiess, having his rifle at the 'present arms', was unable to grasp the ready hand extended to him by the Duke.

It seems that Schiess was still in uniform, although no longer an NCO, and had somehow found his way to India. The EIR Volunteers which proved to be an auxiliary unit, was originally formed as the East Indian Railway Volunteer Rifle Corps whose records are kept in the British Library. On page 544 of the 1884 edition of this publication is a list of the guard staff at Allahabad Station: among the names is F.C. Schiess, but, unfortunately, there are no precise dates for his employment. As late as 1884, therefore, Schiess is recorded in an official directory as being an employee of the East Indian Railway Company and was serving in their Volunteer Rifle Corps. We may never know what took him back to South Africa from India, but there was exactly one year between Schiess being presented to the Duke of Connaught in Allahabad and boarding HMS *Serapis* in Cape Town for his final journey. Whatever happened in this year must have been fairly sudden and dramatic and not the longer, slower decline that was previously believed.

As David Gilmour says in his book, *The British in India*

there were also illnesses and diseases in India that would seldom or never have killed people in Britain…The most common disease for the British was malaria (sometimcs known as jungle fever)… Numerous people died of it when they were in India or after being invalided home to Britain…

Could Schiess have succumbed to an illness such as this? We cannot know from this distance in time. What we do know is that this particular hero of Rorke's Drift never got the opportunity to start a new life in the country that had awarded him their highest military decoration 'for valour'.

Dr Lita Webley supervising Rorke's Drift excavations.

There are no known photographs of Schiess, but Lieutenant Harford, who met Schiess at Rorke's Drift, described him as 'wearing earrings' and 'a very small man with the cut of a seafaring man, which I expect was his real calling'.

Postscript: Lieutenant Chard on Schiess at Rorke's Drift
Chard, in his second report, recorded he had witnessed Schiess, in the midst of the fighting, take careful aim on some of the enemy who were causing problems. Directly on the other side of the wall a Zulu fired almost point blank and blew Schiess' hat off.

During official archaeological excavations of the Rorke's Drift site from 1998 to 2000 a hat badge with a hole the size of a musket ball was unearthed by the senior archaeologist, Dr Lita Webley, at the point defended by Schiess. This item is currently on display at Rorke's Drift Museum.

Acknowledgments

I gratefully acknowledge the assistance and permission of Peter Duckers, to use his original Schiess draft prepared for the *Anglo-Zulu War Historical Journal*. I also acknowledge the use of the Harford quotation, about Schiess, which is taken from David Payne's *Harford*.

Index